THE UNHEALED WOUNDS OF MY FATHER

A Memoir

EMILE MAXI

THE UNHEALED WOUNDS OF MY FATHER

A Memoir

—.—

A Reflection On Trauma, Domestic Violence And Grief That Plagued The Life Of The Author, And How He Overcame It All

—.—

A Book That Seeks To Inspire And Motivate You To Success Inspite Of The Odds In Your Life

—.—

EMILE MAXI

 FriesenPress

One Printers Way
Altona, MB R0G 0B0
Canada

www.friesenpress.com

ISBN
978-1-03-831575-5 (Hardcover)
978-1-03-831574-8 (Paperback)
978-1-03-831576-2 (eBook)

1. BIOGRAPHY & AUTOBIOGRAPHY, PERSONAL MEMOIRS

Distributed to the trade by The Ingram Book Company

Dedication

This book is dedicated to all those who have suffered any form of abuse that might have hindered them in life yet are determined to soar to their highest potential.

Table of Contents

Acknowledgements

To my wife: June Maxi. Thank you for your love, your support, and your encouragement.

To my daughters: Juneile and Nicole. Thank you for your unconditional love and support.

To my siblings: Suze (deceased), Rosana, Ascencio and Mathurine. Thank you for everything, I can't ever repay you for all that you did for me.

To all my nephews and nieces: your parents are amazing. Your parents are the wind beneath my wings and that's why I am now able to write.

To my dear friend: Jean Claude Dorval. Thank you for all the time during our teenage years you spent breathing life into me and giving me hope that God will, one day, make me ride on high mountains. He indeed did! This now gives you the title of a prophet. You saw what I didn't see! I hope there are still friends around like you!

To all my friends and readers of this book. Thank you for your support!

Introduction

For most of us, the cycle of abuse began at home. We became used to it until we allowed it to shape our lives. We allowed it to define us. We acted like what we were told we were or looked like.

God created us for greatness, but we allow someone else to tell us otherwise. We are fooled to believe what or who they say we are. It messes us up for life until we decide to prove them wrong.

At times, the things that were said to us or about us devalue us so much to the point where we try to seek validation elsewhere or try to fit in. We end up in the hand of the wrong person, making wrong choices and the cycle of abuse continues.

To pull yourself from the rubble of life, you must believe that you are a pearl of great value. Your creator God is so particular about your worth. To ensure that you can never be compared with anyone else or devalued because of competition, He created only one of YOU. You are that PEARL!

Let no one tell you otherwise!

PEARLS are not found easily! Deep sea diving is required!

This is what this book is about!

Dive in!

CHAPTER 1
The Odds of Life

———•———

"People are changed only when pushed by pain or when pulled by a vision."

Emile Maxi

———•———

Life's Journey

Life is made of odds. To accept this truth as a fact of life constitutes the very first and undeniable step to emotional healing and eventually to a fulfilled life. Similarly, failing to accept it; is the very first and unstoppable step toward a slippery slope of emotional trauma which will affect everything you do including the quality of your life. What is an odd, you may ask? Let me give you the definition: An odd is the probability that whatever we had planned for or had hoped for may not turn out to be the way we had thought of or anticipated it to be.

I was talking with a friend some time ago and he said to me:

"The odds are against me this week!"

I very well knew the meaning of his statement, but I wanted him to unpack it so that I could help him navigate these odds.

"What do you mean by that?" I asked.

He replied, "Everything feels like it's turning against me. It does not matter what I do and what I try, I am faced with difficulties beyond my control."

Do you ever feel like that sometimes?

Let me be the first to say, "Oh yes, far too many times to count!"

Let me now ask you; who is exempt from the odds of life? If you answered, "No one!"; you are right!

Regardless of how we plan our life, nobody is exempt from the odds of life. All breathing and living souls will face their own odds countless times in their lifetime, however the real issue is not so much the odds but rather our attitude towards these odds. We ought to be prepared to deal with them in a very strategic and rational way.

To get you to deal rationally and strategically with yours, let me ask you; what could be the odds that are against you right now?

Tick off any of the list below that applies or apply to you! Could it be:

- A sweet romantic relationship you once cherished and for some reasons beyond your control it turns sour?

- The dream you once had to have a family and have a child, but somehow it never materialized?

- The dream you once had to raise your children to be respectful, loving, successful and good citizens only to see them choosing a path contrary to what you had hoped for?

- The dream job you once had which you lost due to ill health or due to some internal conspiracy?

- The business venture you embarked on, in which you invested all your savings and energy only to end up broke, in mental exhaustion and causing you to nearly loose your life or damage your treasured relationship in the process?

- The dream retirement you hoped for, worked hard to prepare for, and when you finally reach that moment, only to be hit with ill health that prevents you from enjoying the fruits of your hard labour, or realizing that you can't afford to retire due to financial constraints which force you to work longer than expected?

- The friendship you invested so much time and effort in, only to be betrayed by that friend?

- The marital relationship you cherished so much only to have ended up in a bitter divorce?

- A loved one who ended up having a terminal illness and due to that person's ill-health, it causes you to grieve their loss even though they are still alive?

- That unexpected death of a loved one who went far too soon?

- Or, the fact that you have always taken care of yourself only to have been hit with some health issues that may threaten your independence?

Could it be…? You fill in the blank.

Life is indeed made of odds, don't you think?

- Did you ask for them?

No!

- Has anyone ever planned for them?

No!

- Do we ever want them?

No!

- Do they come without invitation?

Absolutely!

- Can we prevent them?

We wished we could!

If we could, for sure we would prevent them but unfortunately, we can't.

That's why they are called the odds.

They are beyond our control.

They are contrary to the way we had planned our lives.

They come from the opposite path. They are the winds from the opposite direction that prevent us from moving at a normal pace.

They come like a whirlwind ready to suck us out.

They are against the natural flow of the course of our lives.

Can the odds prevent us from moving forward?

Yes, they can, but only if we allow them to!

They can slow our pace, but they can't stop us from pursuing happiness and success - if we arm ourselves with the following:

1. An awareness of their existence

2. A positive mental attitude.

3. A spirit of resilience.

4. A desire to explore a new path.

5. A strong will, not to go against the odds but to work with the odds.

Personally, that's what I have found to be very helpful as I navigated against the odds in my life.

The fact in this journey is that everyone wants to be successful, and everyone craves a fulfilled life. Unfortunately, not everyone will achieve this. Some will! Some won't!

There is no middle ground.

Some will succeed and enjoy a successful life because they are not living in denial. They accept the odds of life. They don't work against the odds; they work with the odds. Some won't soar to the height of their inner potential because they are crushed by the odds. They refuse to accept the odds of life. They will fight against them rather than work with them.

The odds are there to prove what kind of material you are made of. They are like the strong current of the sea or a river. You can't swim upstream or against the current for long without getting fatigued. If you do, it will quickly overpower you and pull you in its direction. You must find ways to go under the waves or ride the waves to remain in the water. This comes with an attitude of resilience.

This is not determined by your social class, the color of your skin, your country of origin nor is it determined by your genes.

It all has to do with the five pointers I shared with you above! At least, that's what I found to be effective for me which carried me through life and its many challenges.

Hold on to your seat! I will soon share with you the brutal story of my life!

Those who do soar, they soar against the odds around them. They muster all their courage and energy to soar because that's what it takes.

There is a great phenomenon that happens every autumn usually between September and November, *the great salmon run*. Salmons are often born in freshwater rivers, then go on to spend a few years in the Atlantic or Pacific Ocean before returning to the very rivers they were born to reproduce.

This journey back home is never an easy one, but necessary to fulfill their innate purpose. During this return from the sea to the fresh northern rivers, they will encounter obstacles such as bears, bald eagles, even fishermen. Travelling up to 1400 kilometers, they will often refrain from feeding using up every ounce of energy they have to swim upstream battling strong currents and rapids. Despite these challenges and obstacles, salmons embark on this journey year after year to ensure the survival of their young.

Those who can't soar, won't soar because they find all the reasons to blame someone or something for their clipped wings. They put the blame on the very element that can help them develop their inner stamina, mental strength, and resilience to achieve great things.

The formula to success or to a fulfilled life is not to find reasons why you are not successful or why your life is not fulfilled but rather to explore new ways against your odds. When it comes to the odds, you must find the will to soar against life's elements. They are here to stay. They won't go anywhere. You must make up your mind to deal with them!

The Game Changer

In my first book: *The Will to Heal,* I began the very first sentence of the very first paragraph of the very first chapter with this statement:

"The *will.* Nothing happens without it. Everything starts with it. It's the only effective tool required to move you out of any situation. God Himself requires it to move you forward, and it's only effective and most powerful in the hand of its owner. The *will* to be and the *will* to do! The second is like unto it: *attitude.*"[1]

To make it in life against the odds of your past, present and future hurts, disappointments, and failures, you need to stop casting blame. You need to take full ownership of your own destiny. Don't make yourself a victim. Turn yourself into a victor. Everything else will follow! It will come at a price, but you must be willing to pay that price.

That price is a determination to turn every misfortune into a fortune. It is a drive to never allow yourself to be down too long in self-pity, contemplating the mistreatments of others, the "this" and the "that" which will paralyze you and clip your wings.

Never allow yourself to see failures as a failure but rather as part and parcel of success, its twin sister. See it as an opportunity to learn, unlearn, and relaunch. The only time you should consider your failures as a failure is – if you fail to learn from them. Make them your teacher. In fact, we learn far more from our mistakes than we learn from our successes.

Never allow yourself to be ill-treated or to dwell in the name calling or the abuses to the point where you allow the mistreatments to define who you are and prevent you from becoming who you will be.

Defy the odds!

You may not have been the architect of your past, but you must now become both, the architect, and the engineer of your future. You must not simply design it, you must also build it, of course, with the help of the well-meaning people in your life.

Get this; no one can really build you up except you! Similarly, no one can tear you down without your permission! Therefore, grant no one that permission!

The Innate Desire

There are two desires that reside within us:

- The desire to soar like an eagle.

- The desire to remain a stick in the mud.

What's the difference between the two?

- The desire to soar like an eagle involves effort.

- The desire to be a stick in the mud involves comfort.

Unfortunately, for most of us, we find comfort in the pain of the past, remaining "sticks in the mud" resistant to change.

We use our past as dress rehearsals - acting as if we are getting ready for a play only to get caught in our own dramatic downfall without ever performing. The more we talk about it, the more we dwell on it. We are not prepared to pay the price to change, so we allow the wind of circumstances to clip our wings. We can't soar with this mindset.

Some cannot endure the pain of climbing the mountain. They prefer to take the elevator rather than the stairs. They prefer to take the shortcut rather than the long route. They fail to realize that taking the shortcut often cuts them short of learning opportunities and building stamina that will be developed by climbing, which will allow them to get to the top and stay at the top.

What helps an eagle to soar? The wind, even though at times contrary in the eagle's ascent!

What does it take for an eagle to soar?

Everything! Every ounce of energy!

What causes an eagle to glide?

The same wind that was against it – the odds!

Similarly, the same wind that was against you will be the same wind that will allow you to glide. It will become the wind beneath your wings. It will become your vantage point for you to see what others can't see because they failed to pay what it costs to soar.

Really, your misfortunes are your fortune seen from different lenses.

All birds can fly, with a few exceptions, like ostriches, kiwis, and penguins.

But not all birds can soar as gracefully as an eagle.

One Friday afternoon, during the Covid-19 pandemic, my wife, June, and I witnessed one of the most important and fascinating lessons one can only get in a tranquil, remote countryside.

But we were not living in the countryside. We were, at that time living in Winnipeg, Manitoba, Canada, not too far from the international airport. Therefore, it is very rare to see eagles in the sky in such a busy city.

These creatures like tranquility, hence, they avoid anything noisy worst, being near an airport, that's not the airspace they would prefer.

One would never see wildlife let alone see an eagle soaring over such a place in the early part of 2021, but, due to the lockdown during the pandemic and the fact that it was quiet and peaceful not to mention less pollution, it was reported in the news that we were seeing some animals and birds that were never seen in the city since their natural habitat were destroyed to make room for human habitat and development.

Sometimes when I go for a bike ride, I would encounter little creatures like foxes, others would report to the news of having the unwelcomed visits of black bears and deer in their neighborhood.

To our delight, my wife, and I saw two eagles soaring over the city of Winnipeg. We were elated. It was a beauty to behold. We had read that a mature bald eagle has a wingspan of about 7 feet and 6 inches when flying or soaring. That's more than my height,

I am six feet and one inch, so you can imagine how majestic these flying birds were.

How can such a big bird fly so high making it the only bird that can fly above the stormy clouds to avoid the rain?

How is that possible?

It is possible only because the eagle does not know that it is impossible!

The word impossible does not exist in its little brain. It does what needs to be done - soar and soar gracefully.

If an eagle can soar, led only by instinct and with less intelligence than you and me, why can't we?

Some will have the desire to soar but will never be able to soar. Some will soar but will never reach the zenith of their full potential.

Why?

> It takes far more than a desire to soar, it takes the will.

> It takes far more than the will to soar, it takes a positive mental attitude.

It takes far more than a positive mental attitude to soar, it takes focus.

It takes far more than focus to soar, it takes resilience.

It takes far more than resilience to soar, it takes the right mindset.

It takes far more than the right mindset to soar, it takes the right environment.

These are what we need to soar against the odds of life!

In the process of soaring to the highest height of its ascent, an eagle will do it with determination, grace, and focus. You too, in the process of soaring to the highest height of your personal and professional ascent, you need to do it with the same attributes, determination, grace and focus.

You can't and you shouldn't allow the elements of nature to deter or distract you from soaring to higher heights. You can't, nor should you allow failures, setbacks, disappointments, emotional abuse, physical abuse, verbal abuse, financial abuse, financial constraints to clip your wings.

You were created to soar! So, soar!

Soar, you must! But do it gracefully!

There are so many who see great potential in you. Far beyond your past and current pain and suffering. They see greatness in you! If you allow them, they will help you pull the best from within. They will inspire you to soar to heights you never dreamed you could reach. Remember, they can only inspire you to soar, but they can't soar for you. The work is yours to do.

As you are reading this book, chances are you either have great dreams and aspirations, you are starting out in your career or you are already settled in one but, your wings are clipped by life's unforgiving pair of scissors.

You might be experiencing a setback. Don't lose hope! You must be strategically prepared to soar. It will not come by chance! It will only come by working hard and smart!

Regardless of where you are in this journey of life made of odds, you are called to rise above your circumstances. You are called to make a difference.

You can only make a difference if you think and act differently.

You are called to soar, not alone but to take others with you.

As you start soaring, you will soon discover that there are others in the horizon, just like yourself, who are trying. Encourage each other. There is enough space in the sky for all of us.

Crush no one in the process of soaring!

As you are climbing on the ladder of success, always resolve in yourself that you will never put down, nor destroy anyone in the process but rather you will leave footprints for others to follow.

You may never know; you may have to either use others' footprints to tread forward or you will need others' footprints on your way down. It pays to soar gracefully. Otherwise, the descent may be fatal!

During my observation of the eagle soaring, my gaze was so fixated on that first eagle, I was so fascinated with the sight of how graceful it was soaring and how wide its wingspan was across the sky, that I failed to see that there was another eagle that was at an even higher altitude until my wife, pointed it out to me. It was so beautiful to watch. Now two eagles, flying to a height that only few birds can fly, observing the landscape down below. That was their vantage point!

Another impressive bird is the Ruppell's griffon vulture. It's recorded that this vulture is the highest-flying bird in the world. It can fly up to 37,000 feet above sea level. That's about the height which most commercial passenger jets will cruise. That's way, way up in the firmament! That's where you belong! That's your cruising altitude!

Can you get to that altitude?

Oh, yes, you can!

You will get to that altitude if you change your attitude!

CHAPTER 2
Rising Above the Odds

———•———

*"No hindrances can handi-
cap you if you have the will
to succeed, the attitude to
get to your desired altitude
and the tenacity to achieve
the unachievable."*

Emile Maxi

———•———

A s a society, we have become increasingly obsessed
with the acquisition of material things. The insa-
tiable thirst for a position of authority drives some
people insane. The notion of fair play has gone out
through the window. The concept of justice for the
less fortunate is increasingly becoming uncommon.

Therefore, climbing the ladder of success becomes more difficult.

To climb, one must either know someone or knows someone who knows someone in authority. At times, it comes with strings attached.

To this, there is a call for change.

Who can make that change?

You can! Attach no strings to it!

While you are climbing, take someone with you. When you get to the top, do not forget where you are coming from, and who helped you get there!

As we begin this chapter, let's reflect on the following questions?

- How can someone who is marginalized, abused, and overused rise to a higher level?

- How can someone who is tagged as "cheap commodity" become an asset of great value?

The answer to these questions is simple. It takes someone outside of himself or herself to see that worth and is willing to make that investment.

Who could that investor be?

Could it be you?

This type of investment can take many varying forms. It can be:

- A word of encouragement to someone who is discouraged,

- Giving someone an opportunity to have a start in life,

- Providing mentorship to someone in need,

- Providing a scholarship to a child in need,

- Or, providing a hot meal to the less fortunate.

To offer a helping hand to someone who is in the ditch of life, you must be standing on a higher ground. Your higher ground is your vantage point - your opportunity to make a difference in that person's life.

It doesn't always have to be financial help. Both of you may be in the same ditch, but you may possess a higher spirit or a different mindset.

You will never be forgotten for any act of kindness extended to someone in need. You may never be repaid by that person, but it will come back to you in some other form. Your children and grandchildren may even reap the fruits of your kindness.

It pays to be kind.

Never miss an opportunity to extend kindness. It's like a real estate investment, it appreciates over a period of years. Your children and grandchildren will thank you for it.

I have been at both ends of the spectrum. I know what it's like! If I can write books today, it is because of people who gave me a sense of self-worth when I thought I was worthless.

Initially, I decided to give this book the title – The Will to Soar Against the Odds. As I began writing, I changed the title to – *The Unhealed Wounds of My Father* based on what I hoped to achieve in terms of what I wish, you, my readers, gain from reading this book.

You may be asking why I changed the title?

The answer to this question will be the subject of every chapter of this book.

Throughout this book, I will share a little of my life story with you, my odds, how I overcame them and how you can overcome yours.

By sharing my own pain with you, you now become aware that you are not alone.

This gives you a sense of a community – At least, a community of grievers - with the will to heal.

My sole reason for doing this is to help heal emotional wounds in the world, one person at a time! Right now, you may be that person.

My Father – His Dreams and His Legacy

My father's name was Ascencio Maxi. He was born in the 1920's in Haiti. His name depicted his mission on this planet earth. If you pay attention to the first few letters of his name, you would have picked up that his name is a derivative of the word "ascend or ascent." So, growing up, I recalled him repeatedly sharing with me the meaning of his name – The one who ascends!

To avoid giving this term "ascend or ascent" a divine connotation, he would rather use the term "the one who rises."

Reflecting on that term, I never asked him, "rising from what?"

From observation and interaction with his siblings and other family members, I know he was coming from a life filled with odds, struggles and a dysfunctional family. Therefore, he held a lot of potential to cause serious emotional damages to his family due to unresolved emotional issues and inter-generational trauma.

However, because he was ambitious and a hard worker, he managed to become a successful business-man in his village. He got married to my mother, Rosana and they began a family. This union produced five children, three girls and two boys of whom, I am the youngest.

My father believed in education. He did not only invest, at least, in the initial stage, in the education of his children, but also in the education of the less fortunate in his village. He ensured that any child seen on the street during school days be interrogated as to why they were not in school. If money was the problem, he would guarantee that the parents get some assistance with their children's school fees to ensure that they are kept in school.

Words Of Wisdom

The wise man Solomon says:

> "Cast your bread upon the waters, you will find it after many days.
>
> Give a serving to seven, and even also to eight,
>
> For you do not know what evil will be on the earth."[1] Ecclesiastes 11:1, 2.

I didn't know the meaning of these verses until several years later, in my teenage years and in my adult life when people who were the recipients of my father's act of kindness, would show kindness towards me for what my father did for them and their children. Even my father, benefited from the kindness of some of these people who remembered how he helped them.

When I lived in Montreal, Quebec, home to one of the largest French-Speaking Haitian communities in North America, upon introducing myself, the mention of my last name would propel someone to ask if I am related to Ascencio Maxi. A "yes" to their question would attract lots of favours to me for which I am very grateful to my dad.

My father was not a perfect man. As I will share with you throughout this book, he inflicted a lot of emotional damage on me which left serious emotional scars in my life, but I must thank him for his act of kindness to others.

I want you to understand that the purpose of writing this book is not just to provide a literary exposé of my life but to help you to reflect on your imperfect parent, caregiver, or spouse. Yes, they made lots of mistakes, but if you can, I want you to reminisce on the good he or she did for you or the good he or she did for others that turned out to be a blessing to you.

When I do grief recovery sessions with people who experience loss of any kind, particularly, a bad relationship with a parent, a spouse, a sibling, or a child, part of the process of the recovery component on a relationship graph is what John W. James and Russell Friedman call "Enshrinement and Bedevilment."[2]

The term "enshrinement" is exemplified by way of an appearance of fond memories and positive comments while avoiding speaking about the bad side of the relationship.

"Bedevilment" on the other hand, is the opposite of "enshrinement." In that, you have a litany of complaints about the person.

When reviewing your relationship with the person, you are unwilling to let go of the pain, the mistreatment, the emotional, the psychological, the financial, and/or the spiritual abuses inflicted on you by the person. Therefore, you find all the reasons to justify your anger towards that person.

Is It Possible to Let Go?

When thinking of your relationship with your parents, you must be willing to look at the good, the bad and the ugly. Understanding that, they gave you what they had – that includes, the emotional scars that they inherited from their parents. But you don't have to pass this bad emotional inheritance to your children. It must stop with you, you must work on yourself and let it go!

Therefore, to be able to let go of the hurts, the emotional pain and anger, you must be willing to analyze and complete the cycle of your relationship with that person – the good and the bad!

My father was not a perfect man, therefore, he inflicted on me his imperfection.

If I don't deal with his imperfection in me, the probability of me passing it on to my children is inevitable.

To avoid that, I must look at the things he did that left emotional scars in me. Be aware of them so that I don't perpetuate them.

Like my father, I am not perfect, therefore, to be able to allow my children to grow in an environment of mutual love and respect, I had to do everything in my power to overcome the things that overcame him.

Reflecting On Your Own Father or Mother...

Your father and your mother were not perfect. They may have done things to you that have left you emotionally shattered. Let me remind you that you are not broken. The only person who can break you is you – your attitude towards the way your father or your mother treated you.

You need to get the hurts out of your heart before they hurt you.

While, in this chapter, I am introducing my own journey with my father, I lingered on the emotional pain he inflicted on me for so long that it affected me for most of my life, until I learned how to heal my own emotional pain.

It used to bother me when I received the favours of others because of the act of kindness of my father to others, while he was so cruel to me. Then, I learned to be thankful for the fact that, at least there was good in him – though I was not the recipient of that good.

It led me to the notion of awareness – I became aware that my father's hostile behaviour and the way he treated me had a root.

I may not be able to find that root, but I need to stop it from taking roots in me. If I don't, it will affect me as a husband and as a father.

I needed to accept the fact that I can't change my father, but I can change my attitude towards him.

I can't change my father, but I can change myself.

Therefore, I needed to complete my relationship with him.

The day I completed my relationship with the pain caused by my dad, was the day I started living.

How did I complete my relationship to the pain so that I am no longer a victim?

You will find the answer as you read this book.

My plea to you is that you work on your own painful emotional wounds, inflicted on you by your father or your mother.

If you don't, it will affect the way you parent.

It will affect your relationship with your spouse.

You need to work on your own emotional wounds.

To properly heal that wound, you need to cut it open. It will be painful in the process but that's the only way you will get the bad stuff out.

This is different than complaining. This way, you are not complaining. You are constructively addressing your unresolved issues to bring them to a state of being resolved.

It means, you can do it whether the person is dead or alive. It's not about them – it's about you.

If you do, you will eventually become a better parent, a better spouse, and a better friend. By extension, society will become a better place because of the new you.

The Start of the Process of Healing Begins with Addressing the Emotional Wounds Properly

Allow me to play my role as your Grief Recovery Specialist just as I have done for others in addressing their own emotional wounds.

Some years ago, I had vertigo. I did not know what it was. All I knew was that everything around me was spinning.

I felt so sick!

I was alone at home but having a small window of "feeling better", I eventually drove myself to the doctor and she confirmed that it was vertigo. Later, I found a physiotherapy clinic that also specialized in vertigo treatment. The Physiotherapist told me: "to heal the vertigo, I must bring on the vertigo."

You see, as long as I kept my head in one position, I was relatively fine, but the moment I turn my head to the right or to the left, it's like everything was crashing down on me.

That feeling was terribly awful!

So, she asked me to sit on the examination table, she held my hand to my chest with one hand and rest her other hand at the back of my head for support and then she pushed me to lie down while looking at the movement of my eyes to help determine if it is indeed vertigo.

Once confirmed, she gave me some simple exercises to do to cause the misaligned beads, called otoconia, in my ears which created the imbalance when they became dislodged, to go back to their places. With these simple exercises, I was back to normal within a matter of two days.

Similarly, to heal your own emotional wounds, you need to bring them back to your conscious memory, the things that your father or your mother did or say to you that caused you much emotional pain.

The same principle applies if it were your spouse.

Just like my past vertigo, it will trigger emotional reactions that will be painful – don't suppress your emotions. Allow your tears to flow! By doing it, you will begin to take control of your emotional life.

Healing Your Own Wounds – Emotional Freedom Exercise

On a separate sheet of paper or in your journal, begin to narrate the incident by writing down the following:

- Your age at the time of the incident

- Where were you when it happened?

- How did it happen?

- What triggered it?

- What was said to you that affected you the most?

- What was done to you that affected you the most?

- Have you ever spoken to someone about it?

- Have you ever spoken to them about it?

- If yes, what was their reaction?

- Have they shown remorse?

- Have they apologized to you?

- Have you forgiven them?

- Who is being hurt the most because of their ill-treatment to you? You or them?

- If you have not forgiven them, how can you find it in your heart and in your best interest to forgive them for your own emotional well-being?

This can also include what they didn't do to care for you, to protect you or to provide for you.

This exercise is intended to free you rather than to enslave you.

This is something that I have found to be very helpful to me as I dealt with my own relationship or the lack thereof with my father.

Though dead a long time ago, the brutal memories lived on in my life and haunted me for a long time. The result of this exercise is liberating though painful.

Regardless of the painful memories, you must rise above the odds of life – if you must enjoy meaningful relationships with your loved-ones.

You owe it to yourself to work on yourself to heal yourself from the inside out!

CHAPTER 3
Traumatized, Who Isn't?

—·—

"Trauma can't be healed until the traumatized has a desire to be healed."

Emile Maxi

—·—

The statistical data is alarming. As parents and caregivers, we undervalue the lethal effects of harmful movies and TV shows on our children. The things we allow our children to watch on television not only predispose them to trauma but also silently traumatize them. Their negative actions later in life are only a replay of the violent acts that their brains captured during their early years. Then, when we see the re-enactment of violence in our society, we disassociate ourselves from them while we are part and parcel of these atrocities.

It is reported that "the average American child watches twenty-eight hours of television a week, not counting rented movies or video games."[1]

In his book, *I Don't Want to Talk About It*, Terrence Real tells us: "by the time a boy is eighteen he has watched an average of twenty-six thousand television murders almost all of them committed by men."[2]

It is very alarming to read the longitudinal study of Psychologist, Leon Efron which was conducted in the late 1950s, but the results of that study were not reported until 1980. In this longitudinal research, he followed 875 eight-year-old children in rural New York state. This is what his longitudinal research revealed:

> "the single best predictor of how aggressive a young man would be when he is 19 years old was the violence of the television programs he preferred when he was 8 years old."[3]

As boys, we liked to watch those action-packed television programs only to realize that they turned most of us into actors of violence.

Actors of violence against other men who are to be our brothers, who, because of their genetic strengths are called to be strong to protect and to provide for their families.

Actors of violence against the ones who are the fabric of our society, the women in our lives. The ones whom we call – our lovers and mothers of our children.

Actors of violence against the women who are so committed to their families that they would do anything to keep their families together.

Actors of violence against the women who stood behind and beside us to contribute to our success even when they barely have made a name for themselves.

These negative things not only inflict pain to our families, but they also inflict trauma which ends up affecting us all – from the four walls of our residential homes to the width and breath of our society.

Trauma comes in many varying forms and shapes.

My First Encounter with Trauma

My very first traumatic experience occurred when I was five years old. Being the youngest of five children, I was very close to my mother. I was like her purse, as they would say. She went nowhere without me.

However, I recalled, one day, she told me that she was going somewhere, and she was going to leave me with the house helper. A few hours passed and she came back looking sad. My little five-year-old mind was also sad because of her sadness. A few weeks later, she went without me again. This time, when she returned, it was obvious that she was very sick. I was always by her bedside. One day, I woke up, I went to her room, she wasn't there.

Then I noticed, the house was full of people – they were crying!

My mother was dead!

I didn't know what death was all about. A few days later, all I recalled was that all of us were dressed in black, and we were taken to the church. There, I saw, for the first time a long box – in it was my mother!

As a five-year-old boy, I didn't know how to process it. My brother was crying. My three sisters were in inconsolable tears. My father looked like he was in disbelief. The whole church was a house of mourning.

At the age of thirty-five, my mother was dead leaving behind five children to be cared for, by a father who usually acted as an army general with no smile on his face which drove fear in me. I was so afraid of the man!

While I was observing and realizing that my mother was lying in a wooden box for far too long without motion, I now began to understand something was wrong – I started crying!

Before they closed the casket, two men reached out and took me and lifted me. One guy on one side of the coffin and one on the other side. Now suspended in the air, they passed me over my mother's dead body seven times. I vividly remember them talking about it – "We need to do this to prevent her from coming for her last son." Which was the custom of the village where I grew up.

Shortly after, they closed my mother's coffin and the service started.

The worst part was when we got to the cemetery, they lowered my mother into the grave.

Losing my mother so young was an extremely traumatic experience for me. As the custom was at the time, we wore full black for twelve months after the death of mom. Having to live with my father as the sole caregiver, proved to be disastrous from I was five years old until his death.

I must admit, life was never the same since then.

Unnoticed Trauma

Certain experiences of our daily lives may produce trauma. Unfortunately, we fail to realize that we are the ones perpetuating it. Not to mention, we allow our children to watch destructive movies and TV shows that thwart the very fabric of their formative minds.

They grow into adulthood with these unnoticed traumatic experiences that leave them confused. Not knowing how to deal with these confusing thoughts and feelings, they act out the internal unstable emotional and psychological negative emotions in the lives of others which in turn affect the lives of their loved ones, their co-workers and even strangers. Therefore, the whole society becomes traumatized by their actions and the cycle keeps on multiplying itself which at times leads to intergenerational trauma.

The sad part is that, while we are all traumatized by what we may experience, from sexual violence, domestic abuse, gun violence, and war, to name a few, most traumatic experiences start at home by way of domestic violence.

According to the Ohio Domestic Violence Network, in their publication: Trauma-Informed Care – Best

Practices and Protocols for Ohio's Domestic Violence Programs, second edition, 2013, it states:

> "Domestic violence is a pattern of coercive and assaultive behaviours including physical, sexual, and psychological attacks, as well as economic coercion, that adults and adolescents use against their partners."[4]

> "The abuse may trigger a negative and long lasting psychological and emotional reaction which in turn may cause trauma. This traumatic experience impacts our thoughts, feelings, and our behaviour."[5]

So, you ask: "What is trauma?"

Most psychologists and psychiatrists agree that "Trauma is caused by a stressful occurrence that is outside the range of usual human experience, and that would be markedly distressing to almost anyone."[6]

The American Psychological Association defines trauma in this way: "An emotional response to a terrible event like an accident, crime or natural disaster."[7]

It is important to note that when a domestic violence occurs which triggers traumatic experiences in our lives and we fail to address them by using the professional help of those who are trained to help us, we learn to live with them but because their negative effects still haunt us, we take them with us into our relationship with our partners, our families and our relationship with others. Because they mess us up, we in turn end up messing up others. We pass them on! This can also lead to intergenerational trauma.

Volumes of books have been written about it. Some even wonder if we really understand the emotional and behavioral complexity of it. Intergenerational trauma is not just a personal problem, it is also a societal dilemma.

Why?

The answer is very simple, if we have unresolved emotional hurts, the probability of us hurting others is greatly multiplied. Unless we understand and accept it as a fact of life and seek professional help, we continue to not only be victims, but we will become perpetrators, victimizing others and the vicious cycle will never end.

In the jungle, the motto is, eat or be eaten. In the cosmos of hurt human beings, the theme often seems to be, abuse or be abused. Hurting people, hurt people.

Proliferations of Abuses

Abuse has a root cause. It occurs when a person is ill-treated, either emotionally, psychologically, physically, spiritually, or financially and allowing this ill treatment to affect him or her to the point where it triggers an emotional reaction. It is called, anger.

This anger can be active or passive.

If active, it will cause you to lash out lethal words and actions that will inflict emotional pain on others including your loved ones.

If passive, it will cause you to act as a quiet storm, inflicting pains without you or others being able to lay a hold on the source or the cause. Regardless of how it manifests itself, active or passive, it will hurt you and others. It will affect you and meaningful relationships. You will need to get a hold of it before it destroys you and your relationship with your loved ones.

In a nutshell, abuse occurs because the perpetuator of the abuse has unhealed and unresolved emotional wounds. Hence, he or she ends up inflicting emotional wounds on others. This can be knowingly or unknowingly. It can be inflicted, witnessed and or experienced. This is how we end up with intergenerational trauma.

Intergenerational Trauma Defined

Not wanting to leave you in the dark, let me dissect for you the definition of intergenerational trauma.

As you can observe, it is a compound word – inter-generational trauma. Here we see two words, but it is made of three words – inter, generational and trauma.

The word "inter" suggests the following: between, among or amid.

The word "generation" conveys the idea of a group of individuals born and living around the same period.

The word "trauma" conveys the notion of an emotional response to a horrific event that happened to one person or a group of persons at some point in time.

Therefore, when we put a specific word before another, it is known as a prefix. Hence, this prefix, "inter" placed before the word, "generation" suggests that before my generation, something bad happened to that generation that has the potential to harm me. Between that person or a group of persons, there was a traumatic event which triggered off a traumatic emotional reaction and it was passed on from one generation to the next generation.

For example, if you or your partner had a parent who grew up in a very traumatic environment, this may have caused them to take on either a neglectful or authoritative parenting style. More than likely, they would suffer the effects of shame, depression, anger, and other risky behaviours which can manifest in the likes of verbal, physical abuse, and substance abuse when it came to caring for you or their children. Growing up in this environment can cause trauma to a child due to the traumatized parent, and the cycle continues till you decide to break it.

My brother was on his own and fending alone for himself for a few years. I was in elementary school. He was in high school. My self-esteem was down in the mud. I was living at my uncle in-law's house. For a while, my father was not visiting – I don't know if he and my uncle in-law had a fall out, but I hadn't seen him in a few weeks, though I didn't mind his absence, at least, I was at peace, and it was a welcomed break from the physical abuse. By this time, I had known where my brother was living, so I went by him one Sunday afternoon for him to help me with a school assignment – something shocking happened.

I have always admired and had high respect for my brother. Throughout the years living at home with the hostility of our father, we bonded. As a man, I would say that he taught me far more about life than I learned from my father.

I had no one to help me and my school assignment was difficult. Although we were separated for a while due to the brutality of our father which affected the close relationship we once had, I was very happy for the fact that now I knew where he lived and that I could go by him for help.

As he was explaining the assignment to me, I was not getting it. Oh Lord! Before I could have time to process what he was saying, my dear brother started beating me mercilessly. I never expected that at all. I literally froze! He slapped me across my face, and he punched me in my head. Then he found a belt, he started whipping me with it until I saw blood all over my body. His landlord came out and rescued me.

I was emotionally broken! Of all the people, I never expected that from my brother. I never knew how to interpret the action of my brother until a few years ago as I was trying to drain my heart of all traits of negative things that happened to me in the past to relieve and set my heart free from animosity until, I read the book, The Body Keeps the Score by Dr. Bessel Van Der Kolk; in it he says:

"Trauma victims cannot recover until
they become familiar with and befriend
the sensations in their bodies. Being
frightened means that you live in a body
that is always on guard. Angry people
live in angry bodies. The bodies of child-
abuse victims are tense and defensive
until they find a way to relax and to feel
safe. In order to change, people need to
become aware of their sensations and
the way that their bodies interact with
the world around them. Physical self-
awareness is the first step in releasing the
tyranny of the past."[8]

Having gone through so much, I could never
muster up the courage to share the physical and emotional pain that my father inflicted on me while all my
other siblings were scattered all over the country. Even
today, I can't even get myself to talk about some of
the horrendous things that my dad did to me without
choking up.

Even today, although we are all in our fifties and
sixties, the moment we start talking about our father,
it won't take long before the place goes into a dead
silence, or we change the conversation with much
pain, or watery eyes.

When my dear and only brother physically abused me to the point where a stranger – his landlord came to my rescue, it was then I realized the negative effects of domestic violence and trauma. It is passed on from one generation to another. In this case, from my father to my brother.

Although I have never talked to my brother about what he did to me, I forgave him. He learned that behaviour. I love him too much to hold this against him.

Just as my brother repeated the actions my father did, if these emotional wounds are not dealt with and treated properly, you will end up doing the same thing to your own family, loved ones and even to strangers. It will become second nature to you. The sad thing about it is that you may not even realize it until it is pointed out to you. When pointed, it will take humility from within you to admit it and the strong will and determination to work on yourself to bring about a personal transformation.

It's important to bear in mind that although the original traumatic event may not have happened to you initially, you will not just be affected by it in the moment, you will be severely impacted by it through your life.

Therefore, your trauma which is the emotional response to a horrific event ends up traumatizing not just you but also everyone else in your circle and will keep on passing on the emotional hurt from one generation to the next unless you decide to address it.

We wonder why some people behave the way they do, and when their behavior differs from our societal norms and expectations, we label them.

We can't offer a helping hand until we extend an empathizing heart.

A heart that is willing to go beyond their behavior. A mind that is curious enough to go into their past so that we can understand their present behavior. When that happens, that's where emotional healing starts.

When I was growing up living with my father or fighting to survive as teenager, there were days, I woke up in the morning, I was utterly disappointed. I wished I had died in my sleep.

You could not have understood my world until you come and live in my heart full of unhealed wounds.

The emotional, the psychological and the physical pains were too enormous to enjoy life.

After all, there was nothing to enjoy!

Life was not worth living.

Have you ever felt that way?

Don't give up! Better days are coming!

At the very beginning of this book, I started with the notion that life is made of odds. We didn't choose them. We have no choice over them. They come into our lives and change us for the worst – At least, that's how it felt then!

If you are at this point now, don't put this book down!

Stay with me!

Let me accompany you to a higher height.

Yes, you read it right, higher height, higher altitude – That's where you belong!

These things can either make you or break you. Don't let them break you.

Let them turn you into a strong and a more resilient person.

There is a Japanese art form called kintsugi which is the art of repairing broken ceramics using "urushi" lacquer mixed with powdered gold.

When a ceramic vessel is cracked or broken, rather than disposing of it, Japanese craftsmen will seal these fissures with the lacquer adding more value to the original piece. The general philosophy behind this art form is to embrace damage, flaws, and imperfections in life, in this case, a person.

The fire of life will reveal the gold in you.

These are the odds or the negative things that were inflicted on us either by a parent, a sibling, a friend, a bully, a spouse, an illness, or a misfortune.

When they happen, they change us for life. We can never be the same unless we do what must be done to heal ourselves. They can't break you! You are unbreakable!

Those who are dead are where they are now because of these odds.

Those who are still breathing, including you and me, we will encounter these odds every single day.

Unfortunately, even a child that is not yet born will have to face them. No one can escape the odds of life.

To help you understand the odds and the concept of soaring gracefully against the odds of life, allow me to give you further glances and sneak peek view of my own odds in the following chapters.

CHAPTER 4
What Happened to Dad?

—·—

*"Your success doesn't begin
until you accept your limitations,
but never allow your limitations
to limit you."*

Emile Maxi

—·—

Less than a year after the death of my mother, life began to change. In fact, the change came much faster than my five or six-year-old mind could process it.

We were living in a small, safe, mountainous, and beautiful city called Marchand-Dessalines, about 160 kilometers north of Port-Au-Prince, Haiti. In that small city or village, my parents would have been counted among the elites.

Back in the seventies, in a small village like mine, any family living in a two-story building, owned by their parents, with nice "modern" amenities, plus having a business would be considered well off. Not to mention the fact that my father also had his own car – the Opel, I remember him calling it. That was a big deal then because not many people owned a car, at the time!

My three sisters, my brother and I were the centre of attention in the town. The children in the neighborhood would have liked to be where we were and have what we had.

My parents had their own business, and they were known to be very kind to the less fortunate. When my mother died, leaving five children, the town was in shock. Gone too young and too soon, one would say – at the age of thirty-five!

We were devasted!

After mom's death, my father was never the same.

Shortly after, he sold that beautiful house, we all moved to a different city with him with no known social and family network.

My six-year-old brain then could never really understand how life could have changed so drastically "overnight."

My father never owned a house since then. We were renting and moving from one house to the next, each time, the rented house was smaller than the previous. Thinking of it now, it was a forced down-size due to financial constraints until he couldn't even afford to rent a house.

When The Worst Happened

My father who used to be a Seventh-day Adventist Christian, stopped going to church, and got into drinking alcohol and smoking cigarettes.

The episodes of verbal and physical abuse broke loose on us.

As I look back, by that time, I was about six or seven years of age, I could have sensed that there was a missing piece from the puzzle – My father took the death of my mother so hard that he drowned himself in drinking alcohol and smoking to appease his emotional pain and the responsibility of caring for five young children. My mother was the glue that kept us all together, but she was now gone.

As we say in Grief Recovery Support, when grief strikes, it does one of two things – it either brings us closer to God or drives us away from God. In the case of my father, the death of my mother drove him away from God.

He could not fathom how God could have taken his wife away from him at the age of thirty-five and leaving him to care for five children, ranging from five years of age, me, to my eldest sister, Suze, aged thirteen.

Dad's emotional pain was so deep and obvious, one could see it with naked eyes. One could cut through it with a knife.

I believe my father started experiencing a slow death the day my mother died.

Tears became his companion, grief, his best friend and anger, his mode of expression.

As he cried, he would be calling the name of my mother and acting as if she were in front of him – he would be asking "Rosana, why have you left me in this condition.? Why didn't you let me go and you stay with the children?

The flow of his tears would be like torrential rain, no handkerchief could be wide or thick enough to wipe his tears away. It was so heartbreaking to witness how the death of a wife could send a man so deep into the ditch of hopelessness and grief.

As for us children, life came to a total halt. Mom was gone, and Dad became inconsolable and bitter till his final breath.

To cope, during his waking hours, he resorted to alcohol and smoking. When he was drunk, funny enough, he would sing hymns from the Seventh-day Adventist Church hymnal. I recall him crying and singing calling the name of my mother: "Rosana, why couldn't I die first. Why did you have to die first and leave me with these five children? I wished I were the one to die!" He would cry himself to bed and would wake up the next day enveloped in grief, pain, sadness, and despair.

My father's way of dealing with grief was heart-breaking. The drinking and smoking habits did not help at all.

In the Grief Recovery Handbook, John W. James, and Russell Friedman call this a STERB, an acronym meaning – Short-term Energy Relieving Behavior.

We all, at some point or another, develop our own short-term, energy relieving behaviours to help us cope with our loss. Our STERBS can be[1]:

- Food

- Alcohol or Drugs

- Anger

- Exercise

- Fantasy – which includes movies, TV, books.

- Insolation

- Sex

- Shopping

- Workaholism

These are only ways to pacify the emotional pain. In other words, this is another way to find comfort – only to find that it's temporary. It leads to despair and further problems.

If I were to address one of the most lethal of them all, I will tell you that it's anger. "Anger," as a STERB, would destroy you and your loved ones as fast as an atomic bomb.

Anger is the root cause of most, if not all, domestic violence. It leaves our families traumatized for life.

Anger – How It Destroyed My Home

Anger turned my father into a monster.

He became so cruel to us, and I couldn't understand why! The least of things we did as kids would engender brutal beatings until a friend of his or a neighbour built up the courage to come to our rescue.

Although, for most of the time I had a father at home, he never showed me love. He didn't care to model healthy manhood, and fatherhood let alone show me how to become a man, a father, or a husband!

I never heard from the lips of my father the words: Emile, I love you!

I would want to believe that he did love me, but he never said it to me. In fact, the brutal way in which he treated me didn't seem to show that love.

I cannot recall ever getting a hug from my father. Not even once!

The only time I recalled that my dad played soccer with me was shortly after my mom's death. I was then five, going on six. I was playing soccer by myself on the balcony of our house, and he joined in. He kicked the ball, about to score a goal, and I blocked the ball. He got so mad and grabbed me by the throat, pushing me against the railing of the balcony, ready to throw me over the balcony to the ground below. A friend of his who was in the living room upstairs saw what was happening, ran and grabbed me, saving me from falling below. His friend was rather upset with him for his brutal act toward me. I was traumatized! To this day, I still experience traumatic episodes during my sleep due to my father's brutality during my childhood. These are manifested by way of severe nightmares. Although, over the years, I have learned how to control them but depending on the stress of the day, they come unexpectedly during my sleep haunting me.

Thank goodness for grief recovery support and for self-directed trauma relieving techniques, I can help myself through deep breathing exercises before I fall asleep to relax my brain and have a good night sleep or anytime, I feel stressed!

I recall when we moved away from our birth village, to live in another city, a few years later, my older siblings could no longer take the beatings, the verbal and emotional abuse, so they either ran away or dad kicked them out of the house.

My sister, Mathurine, whom I follow in terms of birth position, and I were the only ones left at home with dad. Oh, it was hell on earth! Being the last one, the baby of the family, I was not attached to dad. His stern and mean looks drove me away from him.

He made us pay the price for our older siblings leaving home.

I always felt unwanted and unloved. He didn't seem to like anything about me.

I recall when he could no longer pay the rent and things were so bad financially for him, he had to give up that house. He could not afford to rent anything, so he sent my sister Mathurine, to live with an older lady-friend and he sent me to live with my uncle in-law who was a drunkard just as he was.

By that time, I was about eleven years old. I was on and off school. Life was rough to say the least. I had to provide for myself by doing anything acceptable under the law to make a living. John C. Maxwell, writes in his book, Developing the Leader Within You 2.0: "Leadership is like maturity. It doesn't automatically come by age. Sometimes age comes alone."[2]

I was eleven years old, but I felt like I matured very fast to be able to lead myself.

As you are reading this book, chances are, either you or someone you know might be experiencing domestic violence and trauma.

It could very well be that you are the one inflicting pain and trauma on your family through domestic violence or inflicting traumatic experiences.

My heart is appealing to yours, stop it!

Your heart is broken as the result of – you know what! Go and get professional help to assist you in dealing with your short-term, energy relieving behaviours. Find more constructive and meaningful ways to deal with your problems.

Your short-term energy relieving behaviours are only *short-term* solutions. They are not long lasting. You may have learned this as a coping mechanism from your parents, but the time has come for you to stop the cycle of abuse.

It may have started with your father, your mother or a caregiver and continues with you, but you don't have to continue to inflict the pain to your loved ones. You don't have to pass it on to your family. If you do, you will only continue the cycle of domestic violence and trauma.

You can put an end to it now. Brianna Wiest, author of *The Mountain is You* says this:

> "Maybe you know what your mountain is. Maybe it's addiction, weight,

relationships, jobs, motivation, or money. Maybe you don't. Maybe it's a vague sense of anxiety, low self-esteem, fear, or general discontentment that seems to bleed out onto everything else. The mountain is often less a challenge in front of us as it is a problem within us, an unstable foundation that might not seem evident on the surface but is nonetheless almost every part of our lives."[3]

Whatever your mountain may be, you are given the power to conquer it now!

If you do, you will contribute to making this world a better place.

JUST DO IT!

CHAPTER 5
The Grieving Father

---·---

*"Trauma is what happened,
grief is what lingers."*

Emile Maxi

---·---

The physical, psychological, and emotional pains, scars, and ill-treatments I got from my father cannot be put in a book. It would be far too graphic, anger-producing and heart wrenching for you, my readers, to bear. It affected me beyond imagination. If you are or were the victim of domestic violence and or trauma, I hope you will take the necessary measures to stop it.

Terrence Real, a family therapist, in his book: I Don't Want to Talk About It, says: "It takes three generations to heal from trauma. Your dad (or mother) never made it and you're in the middle. Let's see what bringing your own children can do."[1]

If my father, based on his own trauma didn't heal, I was a victim of his own trauma, I hope I can stop it with my own children.

For a mighty long time, I have suffered emotionally from the traumatic experience of my father's brutality and his anger. I believe my siblings would say the same.

When I was in graduate school, a lot of the psychology classes I took required that we did some kind of reflection on our childhood experiences and at times, the professors would pair the students up to practice on each other and then report to the class. Through these experiences, I was always advised to write a book on my traumatic childhood experiences to help me talk about it and hopefully, it would bring some "relief" and additionally help the wider public through my experience. I always shy away from that because my childhood memories are very ugly and extremely disturbing. There is nothing about it I want to remember, though they are very much vivid in my mind. It's far too traumatic.

After writing my first book, *The Will to Heal*, I must say, writing this book was a daunting task. My wife, June, will tell you that I have had several episodes of nightmares during my sleep – though I am in my fifties. These things hardly go away. I learn how to manage them but depending on what I am dealing with, they show their ugly faces.

The more informed we are about our own traumatic experiences, the better prepared we are to deal with them.

I became a Certified Grief Recovery Specialist not only for me to deal with my own issues but also to help people like you and your loved ones deal with them.

From my personal experience with trauma, I can tell you that trauma is what happened, but grief is what lingers. You can't deal with traumatic experiences in your life until you deal with the grief in your heart.

I like the way Sheleana Aiyama in her book, *Becoming the One,* puts it, in the section, Things to remember, she gives us some good advice to help us work on ourselves. She says:

- "Your relationship with yourself sets the foundation for all the relationships you have in your life.

- The inner work requires that you return to yourself and take radical responsibility for your mind, your emotions, and your reality.

- It's okay if you feel a bit disconnected from your authentic self, right now. Be gentle and practice compassion.

- Rebuilding a relationship with yourself is a gradual process where you learn to witness your thoughts and reconnect to your body and emotions.

- Choosing to heal your relationship pattern is not about fixing yourself; it's about reclaiming your wholeness."[1]

Secret Methods of Communication

All the years we spent living together as siblings, we loved each other's company. Since dad's presence at the house was always regimented and coupled with brutality, we knew that if one of us were somewhere or fail to engage in or do the assigned household shores then, a kick would land on our body or a slap in the face or a piece of wood or a whip would land on our backs, so, to forewarn of such, we developed whistling codes or hand clapping to communicate with each other and to inform each other of dad's presence or attacks.

My two eldest sisters had moved to another city to fend for themselves. Oh, I missed them so much! My brother was still living in the same city, Gonaïves, as my sister, Mathurine and I, but I didn't see him often.

When we were separated and scattered, these secret methods of communication became very useful. Whenever my siblings would show up in the neighbourhood to check on my sister or myself, these codes became the way to locate where they were and the urgency of the beckon call.

I couldn't miss the distinctive sounds of those whistles or hand claps. I could tell from a mile away whether it was my eldest sister, my elder sister, or my brother. Then, I would respond.

The tonality of my whistling or my hand claps would indicate, to them, if my father is around, if he is sleeping, if he is drunk, if he is near me, far from me, or if I am in danger or how soon I can come to meet with them.

Once it's safe, I would find a way to escape to see them. There, they provided encouragement and comfort to me and shared whatever they had brought for me – food or a little cash.

As I am writing and reminiscing on this episode of my life, it brings tears to my eyes.

While away for that brief period, if dad called me or woke up from his drunkenness, calling for me to bring some water or to light his cigarette and I didn't respond or show up within seconds – hell would break loose! He would beat me – give me a knocking punch, kicking me and asking me about the whereabouts of my siblings.

Hope Matters

I always knew that my siblings, though living in another city, were not going to let me live in that hell forever. My little escapes to meet with them during those moments gave me hope.

Hope kept me alive!

They went to make plans for me.

They will come back and get me out of this dungeon of hell.

My siblings were all teenagers but very responsible. I believed in them, and I believed and relied on them for strength.

I knew they had a plan for me.

That gave me hope even in the face of adversity.

My eldest sister, Suze, the first born, who was like a mother to me, she was also my Godmother. I never called her by her first name, Suze. I called her: "Marraine" in French, which translates in English, "Godmother."

As her baby brother, she treated me with motherly love! She cared for me as her baby brother and a son!

We were inseparable!

My two eldest sisters, Suze and Rosana were very close, so they planned for the rest of us to reunite with them in the capital city, Port-Au-Prince.

Occasionally I would see my brother, Ascencio Jr. and my sister, Mathurine. Life seemed to get harder each day. Many times, though only 12 or 13 at the time, I thought of ending my life, because life was far too unbearable living with my father.

If he was around, a day would not pass without me getting some severe beating and ill-treatment. I recall he once didn't give me anything to eat for about two or three days. Dying of hunger, he finally cooked something and called me. I reached for the plate of food he was handing me, as I reached out to take it from him, he landed the steamingly hot plate of food in my face and then he threw it to the dog and told me, if I wanted it, I must partake of it with our domestic dog on the ground, because "that's where I belonged", he said!

I believe the only reason why I didn't take my life was my love for my siblings. I didn't want to turn it into a traumatic experience for them. I knew it would have affected them negatively for the rest of their life. I couldn't bring myself to hurt them that way. I loved them far too much and I knew they loved me too!

However, that didn't stop me from waking up disappointed to see that I was still alive to see another horrible day with my father in the picture.

Eventually, my father sent me to live with my uncle in-law, while he moved somewhere else. He never told me where he was living. However, he often came by to visit my uncle in-law which happened far too frequently during the week for my comfort as his visits would consistently end with him beating me until there was nothing left in me to beat. At times, the beating, and the blows on my eleven-year-old body were so deadly that I would pass out.

The objects he would use to beat me varied in size, forms, and shapes. When his hands were tired, he would kick me to the floor to inflict the worst of damage and pain to my body. Most of the times, he would ensure that the doors are locked to prevent the neighbours from coming to my rescue.

My sister, Mathurine was the only one I had nearby, but I only saw her when I would go to look for her and we would share a brief but meaningful companionship.

Most days, I survived without food, after all I had no one to provide for me as an eleven-year-old. Then, I realized that I had to find a way to survive. I started to skip school to do house chores for people and they would pay me. Later they discovered that when they gave me money for my service, my father would search my pocket and take away my money and then beat me even more, thinking that I did not give him all.

The physical pain that my father inflicted on me are all over my body. They account for the atrocities of his personal trauma which he never dealt with and ended up inflicting them on me.

But the worst of it all, is the emotional pain. The things that he said that devalued me. These things brought me so low that I believed everything he said about me to the point where I allowed his derogatory name calling to define who I was and nearly ruined my life.

Over the years, I have learned a lot from reading books on emotional health. As an adult, while I read the Bible, I soon realized that I needed to read a bit more on a specific field, such as emotional health so that I could address those specific needs.

I used to get unhappy with God because, I would pray and ask Him for help, but then more trouble would come my way.

I would read the Bible for hope, but I was in despair. I had to find more specific things to help me deal with my heartache – though I still relied on the Bible and on God for strength. The literatures on emotional health gave me clear insights and the steps to take to work on myself. I needed more than hope, I needed clear professional guidance on how to deal with my emotional issues.

If you find yourself in the same situation, in as much as you will rely on God for strength and the Bible for hope, you need practical professional help. I suggest the same to you. There are also lots of books on Amazon or your local bookstores to help you. Do not hesitate to reach out to a professional to help you!

One of the great books I have found in this field is written by Philip Newton – Healing from Childhood Trauma: How to Recover from Sexual, Physical and Emotional Abuse. It is a guide and Workbook, so, it's a perfect companion for you and will help you. In the section dealing with the benefits of practicing self-compassion, he puts it like this: "Practicing self-compassion help you to acknowledge your pain/suffering honestly and will help you to heal."[2]

On the outside, you would believe that I am the perfect man but, on the inside, the battle was raging as I tried to convince myself that I am not who and what my father made me to be!

I have learned and used different techniques, Neuro Linguistic Programming is one of them, as they aided me in the reprogramming of my mind, to think more positively about myself instead of the negative attributes my father instilled in me.

For years, though I am a person of faith, I questioned God.

Like many of the Old Testament prophets – The prophet Habakkuk for example, I have asked God many questions for which I have no answers: I asked, God:

"Where were you when all these things were happening to me?"

"Why didn't you stop the violence against me."

"Do you really care?"

"Why don't you stop violence against the weak, the less fortunate and the innocent?"

As I engaged in grief recovery support with grievers, I realized that the same questions seemed to always surface. It became evident that, for someone who was physically abused, it's hard for anyone to convince them of God's protection after the fact.

They often wonder, "if God didn't protect me then, or stopped it from happening, why should I even bother to ask Him for help now?"

In such a case, it is futile to try to play God's advocate. To the person who is hurting, the more you try to spiritualize the concreteness of their reality, the more painful you make it for them.

I find that it's best for me to say that I don't know. It's more reassuring for that person to hear you say that you too have asked the same questions, but you still have not found the answer. At times, silence is even more reassuring.

Let God do the healing Himself!

You are not the healer! Your work is to provide support without judgment or criticism.

If you are the one dealing with this disturbing stuff, let me reassure you that it's okay to ask questions!

Don't feel embarrassed!

Don't allow anyone to send you into a guilt trip when asking these questions.

Questioning is part of therapy.

If you stay in denial, you will never be healed.

God doesn't mind you asking questions! He asks us to reason with him.

Asking is part of reasoning!

Trust me, your healing won't start until you involve God and part of it is asking Him questions.

Let me reiterate, questioning is not just therapeutic, it's part of therapy. Go, unload your questions on Him! Reason with him!

As a Grief Recovery Specialist and a Life Coach, one of the best ways I assist people address the uncertainties of life is by asking them questions. We solve problems by asking questions to clarify our doubts and fear. It provides an avenue for us to reason.

Only two friends can reason together!

God is your friend, although I can't tell you why he allowed certain things to happen.

In grief recovery sessions, I usually say to my grievers, grief does either one of two things:

It drives us away from God or

It brings us closer to God – and if it drives us away and we maintain an open mind and we have open-minded and balanced God-fearing people around you, who will not judge nor criticize us, the probability of us coming back to God or maintaining our faith in God is greater.

The more dogmatic you are, the more difficult you will make it for the griever.

While I still don't have answers to those questions, I do have some insights to share with you toward the closing chapters.

As you have read my questions to God and my issues with God, there is a chance that you might feel the same way. I am not here to cast judgment on you, I am here to support you, not to castigate nor to criticize you.

Your feelings and emotions are real, and I want you to be real with yourself and with the process. All the prophets who remained faithful to God had questions.

You can start with anyone of them – examples, Jeremiah, Isaiah, Habakkuk, and the list goes on!

Go and read about anyone of them, you will hear, not just their questions but also their complaints.

If you are in such a situation, all you need is a compassionate heart, a listening ear and a process to help you deal with it – That's all!

You read my questions to God, I am asking the same of you, don't criticize me for my questioning God.

This is what anyone who went through the hell of domestic violence and trauma needs from you - A listening ear and a compassionate heart!

In fact, because of my traumatic experiences, I find that I am better able to connect and understand those who experience abuse and end up being traumatized by the ones whom they call their parents, siblings or loved ones.

The hardest thing to accept about domestic violence is that they are committed by the ones whom we love and who are supposed to love us and care for us. This is what causes the trauma!

For years, I couldn't get out of my mind, the lethal words of my father:

"A lemon tree is better than you, at least I can get lemons from the tree and make lemonade."

"You are worthless."

"You are an idiot."

"Anything that is worthless must be destroyed."

"You will never become anything in life."

"Bringing you into this world is my greatest mistake."

"A dog is better than you."

Friends, only things that are appropriate for the eyes are mentioned in this book.

For years, I had difficulty looking at people straight in the eyes when engaged in a conversation because my father demanded that I look down when he is talking to me.

If I looked at him straight in the eyes, he would give me some hard blows and punches directly on to my nose until the severity of the pain caused me, twelve or thirteen years old to pass out in a pool of my own blood.

Locked in the dungeon-room with no way to escape, I would call for my dead mother to come for me – for death was better than life!

My brother and my sisters were not with me so I was left alone to endure the pain of my father whose trauma seemed to have had such a strong grip on him that he couldn't deal with it or find professional help therefore, he is releasing the full weight of his trauma and unresolved grief on me.

For years, I had difficulty kneeling to pray because I remembered when my father would strip me naked like the day I was born and beat me until I had bruises, and open wounds everywhere on my body. He would put me to kneel on crude, rough sea salt with my arms stretched like the thief on the cross, then, putting two relatively large stones in the palm of my stretched hands and another stone on my head. He demanded that I maintain balance and ensure that the stones don't fall, while kneeling on the rough, crude sea salt. If I failed to maintain my balance, he would beat me even more until the open and fresh wounds would ooze more blood.

If he is beating me by giving me one hundred lashes, he would ask that I count them. If I count the lashes and I were to miscount due to the pain, he would start back from number one again until I count it correctly.

Often, this meant, I would get double the lashings! Oh, it was brutally unbearable!

Just in case you are wondering why no one called the police. In such a country, at least when I was growing up in Haiti, you don't do that! That's a waste of time. He could have killed me; nothing would have happened!

Life was unbearable, to say the least!

My friend, as you are reading my life story and ordeal through the pages of this book, I don't know if you can identify with any of it. If not, I am very glad for you.

If it's not you, I can almost guarantee it that you know of someone who is being abused by a:

- Spouse

- Parent

- Caregiver

- Supervisor

- Bully

- Child

- A relative

- Friend

- Stranger

You can't afford to allow the abuses to continue under your watch.

If you don't do something about it, you are part of it.

Do your part to stop it!

If you are the one being abused or traumatized, refuse to continue living in it. Or else, you are perpetuating the abuse.

Allow no one to tell you that you should pray about it, stay in it until God takes you out of it!

Far too often I hear this from Christians: "Stay in it until God delivers you. It might be your cross that God wants you to bear."

Let me tell you this, you need no form of abuse in your life.

Get out of any abusive relationship – the day it happens!

You need help!

Seek help from a mental health professional!

Work on yourself!

Unfortunately, far too many children end up staying in an abusive home filled with domestic violence which leaves them traumatized - just because they don't know what to do.

The worst part is that when children witness abuse, they become traumatized. This trauma will affect them for the rest of their lives, if not dealt with.

Unfortunately, they too will end up either in abusive relationships or become abusers. So, let's stop the cycle!

CHAPTER 6
The Great Escape

—·—

"Often, to be free, one must escape. But true freedom is a state of the mind. Your body can't be free until your mind is free."

Emile Maxi

—·—

The domestic violence and the traumatic experience with my father continued until one day, Suze and Rosana arranged, discretely communicated to me through a friend of theirs that I must meet them at a specific time and place. So, I prepared myself accordingly and ensured that no one in my circle knew about it because if it were to be reported to my father, and that plan were to be aborted, he would have killed me.

As planned, as executed! I packed my little bag. Thank goodness I didn't have much to pack – all I had to my name were, two short sleeve shirts, two pairs of short-pants and a worn-out pair of shoes that left me walking almost bear-footed. With that I took off to the place where I was to meet my sisters.

They took me away, we embarked on a bus and relocated to a different city. The plan was to relocate to Port-au-Prince, the capital city of Haiti. We went back to our birth village, first, Dessalines. My sister, Mathurine, and I stayed with my paternal aunt for a while and then at a house next to my grandfather's old house before his death, then finally, to Port-au-Prince, where little by little, we were reunited one person at a time. My eldest sister, Suze was the master mind in all this planning and moving, supported by my elder sister, Rosana.

The moving from one city to the next, from one house to the next were so rapid that I can't recall all the details about the order of the moves. One thing I remember, by the time all of us were totally reunited, Suze and Rosana already had their first child.

My new responsibility was to help take care of my nephew and my niece. A few years later, my brother had his first daughter.

Living Together as Teenagers and Young Adults

We were happily living together with very limited means while trying to make ends meet.

Life began in a different way but still full of challenges for a group of youngsters trying to live like adults in a rented one-bedroom, with most of us sleeping on the floor. This is what happens when you take a leap of faith. As Life Coach, Mike Bayer, in his book, Best Self, puts it, "Sometimes following your authenticity means taking a leap of faith and not fully understanding where it's going to take you."[1]

That's what we did, we took a leap of faith. There was no luxury but there was much love and that's what mattered the most!

There was no food, most of the time, but we were happy to be in each other's company.

As you can expect, there were misunderstandings at times but the sense of purpose and reasoning prevailed – we came from far, we were shattered but not broken, therefore, we were not going to let petty things divide us.

We were resilient and we were going to support each other with the only thing we had – a mindset to thrive and the determination to reach the zenith of our potential with each one cheering on the other to success.

The older siblings worked odd jobs to send the younger ones to school. We cared for each other. Mistakes were made, but we understood that was part of the adjustment. It's all part of life! We agreed to respect each other and to show love although we were not shown how to love. Although we didn't see love in practice at home with our dad, love can be explored because we all had a heart full of love for each other. We forgave each other and kept on pressing on!

From time to time, the issue of past domestic violence inflicted on us by our father and the effect of intergenerational trauma manifested themselves in our midst, but they were quickly identified, and we cried together, and we were determined not to allow them to have any place in our one-bedroom apartment, much less in our heart. We came too far, and we were not going back.

We didn't have any material possession, but we had great love for each other and thrived to respect each other – after all, that's what will get us out of intergenerational trauma and that's what would get us out of poverty.

Suze really took her place as the mother for the rest of us – two girls and two boys. She was in her twenties then, but she led us with love and compassion, receiving much needed moral and emotional support from my elder sister, Rosana.

My friend, remember that I call this a memoir – It means that I am sharing my life story with you. We all have a story to tell! At times, they are far too painful to tell let alone to put it in a book.

When we tell our story, it may be painful, like it is to me now, but it will help you to appreciate your small and humble beginning. It will help you to be thankful for your present accomplishments. It will help you to have compassion for others who are trying. It will provide encouragement to others who may have lost hope but when they hear your story, they will have hope – after all, we all need a little of it.

The Leg in Legacy

When I am with my siblings, we enjoy each other's company but the moment the name of our father is mentioned, dead silence over-takes the room. The domestic violence, emotional pain and the trauma are too deeply seated on our heart. What I have described to you so far is only what's good and mild enough to put in a book.

Have I learned from it?

Absolutely!

I will share all of that with you in the succeeding chapters.

I will never forget that while my siblings and I were living on our own, life was rough, but it was peaceful – if you understand what I mean. I was a teenager in school, so I didn't contribute to the rent neither did I have to contribute to food. Most of the time, I would wake up hungry, walk to school at least ten kilometers away, one way and sometimes, I had to go to bed hungry.

If we could afford to have two meals for the day, it was safer to eat one meal and save the other for tomorrow. That was our reality, and we were grateful for the fact that we had kind-hearted, perceptive, and wise neighbours who, though they too had limited means, knew: "when the cat lies in the coal stove, there was no activity in the kitchen." They shared the little that they had so that we could have something to cook. Bear in mind that, in such a situation, we didn't eat to fill our stomach, we ate to survive. If I had enough to fill my stomach, I would rather eat a portion of it then leave some for later or for tomorrow. That was life!

Looking back, I had a drive to succeed despite all the things I lacked and wanted. As Amanda Dewinter, in her book, *the Success Code – Unlocking Your Potential, Achieve Your Goals*, puts it, "To achieve success, you have to have ambition: the strong desire and determination to achieve it. Success is not going to happen by chance. You have to want it; you have to make a conscious decision to choose it, to take the steps towards it, and be willing to strive for it."[2]

That was the life I lived for about six years until one day, it all changed!

We were living in a new suburb in Port-au-Prince, one day, a friend came to me and said:

"Emile, I saw a man in the neighborhood. You look like him, you walk like him, and you are almost as tall as he is."

By this time, I was about sixteen years old. I was already a tall guy for my age, so the man must have been over 6 feet tall!

I froze!

My heart sank!

My heart was beating much faster than I could process my thoughts!

Who could it be, I asked myself? My friend didn't know that I had a father – alive.

He asked,

"Where is your father?"

I avoided telling him the truth, because I couldn't afford to tell the truth much less to bear the truth!

I was hoping that it was all in a dream, but I believed him! He was one of my closest friends.

A few days later, my friend and I were standing at the entrance of the street one night, he said:

"Emile, there, is the man!"

When I looked up, indeed, *that man* was my father, walking past my street, drunk, barely maintaining his balance.

He looked worn out. He was about a hundred feet away from me.

My heart leaped in fear!

I froze!

I burst in tears! Then, I ran away as far as I could! I didn't want him to see me! My heart was filled with conflicting feelings, but I didn't see myself opening my heart to a life full of physical and emotional abuse while I was trying to reconstruct the broken heart of a teenage boy who had very little social skills due to the absence of a relationship with his father.

That day, I ran away and let my father continue his journey to wherever he was living. I didn't want to have anything to do with him.

The pain and the trauma were ruining my life.

By this time, the nightmares were constant and disturbing during my sleep. I was a broken boy!

My father was broken, so, he broke me!

Lessons from the Mistakes of Others

Let me ask you a question:

"What's the difference between a wise person and wiser person?"

The answer is as simple as this – "A wise person learns from his or her mistakes, but a wiser person learns from other people's mistakes."

So, I want you to learn, not just from your own mistakes but also from other people's mistakes.

I want to let you know that if you are broken, until you fix your brokenness, you will break your children – just as my father broke me.

The person whom you see, may look good and you may want him or her as your partner, as a marriage officer for some thirty-one years now, as of the writing of this book, I will tell you, regardless of the love that you have for each other, unless you seek help to fix yourself, you will end up hurting your partner.

Deal with your intergenerational trauma and the abuses inflicted on you before you commit to a relationship. This will ensure that you don't inflict pain to your partner and to your children.

Don't think that jumping from one relationship to another will solve your problem – you are only proliferating the problem.

If you are already in a relationship and you are still messed up, chances are you are ill-treating your spouse who loves you so much that he or she would be prepared to do anything to seek help for you so that you can nurture a strong relationship. Failing to do that will resolve in continued trauma to your children and to your spouse.

If you are separated or divorced, don't think marrying another person is the solution to your love story.

The problem is innate! You may be a very nice person but the monster within you is greater than you!

To get it out, you need professional help!

The Emotional Wounds

My friend, I must tell you, though my father had a difficult time expressing himself in a healthy way to us, I do believe with all my heart that deep down, my father was a good person.

During the years of his wealth, he fed people. He did so much for others! He was kind! He paid their rent. He sent their children to school. My father was carrying his own trauma that was greater than himself. Unfortunately, he didn't know how to unload it. He didn't know that he could have gotten help. He didn't know how to process it, leading him to express his anger and frustration in the only way he had learned, drowning his sorrows in alcohol and cigarettes - These were the unhealed wounds of my father.

Is this what you really want for your spouse?

Is this what you really want for your children?

Is this the legacy you really want to leave behind?

My Nightmare Episodes

My wife, June, will tell you that since we got married at the age of twenty-seven until now in my fifties, I still have severe nightmares due to the atrocities inflicted on me by my father although he died a long time ago.

Over the years, I have studied, and I have read extensively in the field of emotional health for the sole purpose of healing my broken heart which will also assist me in working with others so that I can help those in a similar situation.

As a Grief Recovery Specialist and Life Coach, I am pleading with you to work on yourself so that you can enjoy a more fulfilled life.

Your spouse will enjoy spending time with you. Your children will not have to tip-toe around you anymore. You don't have to continue to be a victim of your past. There's no need for you to take refuge in the bottle or substance abuse.

There is no solution in the bottle!

There is no solution in the cigarettes!

There is no solution in drugs!

The solution lies within you!

The solution lies in your ability to realize that there is a problem. You may not have created it. It was inflicted on you.

Do you use other substances to help you pacify your problem?

Don't run from your problem. If you do, you will be running for the rest of your life.

You don't need to inflict it to the ones who love you the most.

You are suffering from it!

Your loved ones are suffering from it.!

You are the sole person who can fix it!

So, fix it!

CHAPTER 7
The Unwelcomed Reunion

—·—

"Never miss an opportunity to show kindness for it may be your last."

Suze Maxi

—·—

Life is full of odds! These odds should cause us to reflect on ourselves and our actions. The ones whom you ill-treated yesterday may be the ones who will take care of you tomorrow when the hand of time turns against you.

Since my friend told me about the man he saw, I went into panic mode until I saw the man for myself – it turned out that it was indeed my father.

The day when I saw him drunk, I ran away. I hoped he didn't see me. Although he was drunk, I believe he saw me because he started to frequent the place more often. More of my friends started to tell me about him and that he has been asking people in the neighborhood for our exact address. It was clear that my dad had reached a point in his life where he felt that he needed his children back in his life. We hadn't seen each other for at least five years.

My dad and my eldest sister, Suze always had a soft spot for each other. Since our mother died, Suze was the one whom he relied on to take care of the house and the rest of us. Although she was thirteen when our mother died, she matured very fast to meet the demands of caring for the home.

To us, she was reliable, dependable, accessible, loving, and lovable. As John C. Maxwell puts it: "If you don't have influence, you will never be able to lead others."[1]

Suze had great influence not just on us, her siblings but also on our father. She commanded respect and respect was granted. My father trusted her with everything. When they used to talk, I could see that he had a lot of love and respect for her as his eldest child. However, she was not exempt from the domestic violence, but she did not get as much as we did. I believe

I got the brunt of it all – especially when he placed me to live with my uncle in-law.

The Manifestion of Love and Compassion

When she heard that our father was in the neighborhood and of his condition, she was moved with compassion. Our little bedroom apartment was already cramped with the five of us plus my eldest siblings three children now making it eight of us. Suze wanted to let our father in our little "inn" even after all that he did to us. She strongly believed that was the best course of action.

"Never miss an opportunity to do good – especially when it is your own blood", she would say.

That sister of mine was rock solid as a girl in her twenties. We respected the very ground she walked on!

When she spoke, we all listened! When we heard of his situation, our heart melted within us, and within a matter of days, dad came to live with us. It was a joy to see how he loved and admired his grandchildren. That was the first time I saw him showing love and affection to his own. My father never said to me once, "Emile, I love you." I have never gotten a hug from my father. So, it was nice to see him hugging my nieces and nephew.

I recalled looking at him sitting on a chair by the entrance door of our apartment, it was so sad to see a man who once had it all going for him, now with just a few pieces of clothes to his name. The love that my father was showing to my nieces and nephew was short lived. He didn't learn his lessons – life can be brutal. When we fail to learn the lessons, it's trying to teach us, the consequences can be equally brutal.

In this case, the lesson of life is – love your family. Treat them well. If you fail to do that, the consequences will be very severe.

One day, my father was smoking and watching one of my nieces who would have been two or three years old at the time, while she was playing by herself in the dirt. Being the curious toddler she was, took a handful of dirt and ate it!

As a parent, you know this isn't uncommon for children to do especially at that age. This somehow greatly displeased my father. The same cigarette he was smoking, he landed onto her poor little arm. She screamed and she cried! This led to an altercation with Suze because that was her youngest daughter. As he wound up to punish her, he noticed that if he were to attempt to raise his hand at us, he would have a whole gang of strong people to come down at him. So, he left the house, and we didn't see him again for another couple of years.

The Christmas That Changed It All.

My sister was always a kind-hearted person. She did not hold grudges. She was always quick to forgive. She was beautiful inside and outside!

Christmas in Haiti, at that time, was a time when everyone was kind to each other. Those who had jobs would get their bonuses in most cases, a second pay cheque equal to their month's salary, so kindness was extended to the ones whom they knew in their community were in need. They would give a little cash to the youngsters or to their parents to ensure there's food on the table on December 24, Christmas eve, which was then the most celebrated day of the festive season and January 1, Haiti's Independence Day, which was also a big celebration day in Haiti.

Every home would cook pumpkin soup – to commemorate the celebration of independence and freedom from slavery because, during slavery, only the white masters used to eat pumpkin soup. Therefore, it does not matter where in the world Haitians would find themselves, the tradition is that we would celebrate by waking up early, cook the famous pumpkin soup and feast on it all day.

December 24 and January 1 were the days when, people would cook and share with each other their delicious meals. They would nicely pack and send a meal to a less fortunate or to a friend.

A Father in Need

It was Christmas! Suze, the eldest child, daughter of my abusive, messed-up father, couldn't bear to think that it's Christmas and her father is somewhere without someone to provide him with a delicious home cooked meal.

She seemed to have had a way of tracking his whereabouts. She worked very hard to support us. Our neighbours were also kind in providing groceries for us to ensure that we had food for the season – I thank them for their kindness!

Being the youngest child, the lot would always fall on me to do the chores. So, Suze asked me to take the food to my father. Being the eldest and I am the youngest, I couldn't bear to say no to her. So, I agreed!

She gave me the instructions as to how to get there. It was a far way off, on the complete opposite side of town. I had to take two taxi cabs to get there. My sister somehow always had a way of communicating with my father despite us not having a telephone, so it was no surprise she knew where to find him.

When I got off the taxi, my father was there waiting. He took the well-packed thermos-like box with multiple layers of bowls containing different dishes. He snatched the box from me and demanded that I get back aboard the next taxi and leave. I was so afraid!

He looked angry!

He looked drained!

He looked disturbed!

He looked hungry!

I told him that I wanted to go to his house with him and spend a little time with him since we haven't seen each other in a couple of years.

It was the first time; I experienced deep sadness and compassion for my father.

It was the first time; I saw the weight of a life-long trauma in my father's eyes.

Suddenly, I experienced a deep sense of love for my dad which I had never felt before due to the emotional pain and trauma he inflicted on me.

It was the first time; I experienced for myself, at the age of seventeen nearly eighteen years old, the weight of inter-generational trauma in the life of my father.

He was trying to protect me from something, but it was far too late – I had already seen it all.

His life of emotional pain was written all over him and the ink of his life of trauma had already been running all over the canvas of my life and tainted the very fabric of my being.

His pain became my pain!

His trauma now becomes intergenerational – from him to me and if I am not careful – from me to my children, his grandchildren.

For the first time, I confronted my father:

"I am not leaving, Daddy!"

"I need to know where you are living!"

For the very first time, my soul connected with the man who had been a monster to me all my life.

At that moment, I felt I needed to connect with my father at a deeper level.

I grew up motherless. I learned in later years, from aunts, uncles, and other community members that my father was abusive to my mother even a few weeks before her death.

Life was never the same without my dear mother! She was only thirty-five years old when she died. I was five years old when she left me in this misery!

Could it be that my father was broken, before he married my mother? Therefore, broke her in the process?

Could it be that my father didn't know how to seek help to fix himself emotionally and that he ended up breaking me as well?

As I was standing there, he was still demanding that I leave – it all happened within a matter of minutes.

The more he demanded, the more my eyes pierced through his soul to see his pain. The more I felt the desire to connect with him and to help him – After all, he is my father, said my compassionate heart!

Finally, I realized that I couldn't, and I won't win this battle against him as he started to raise his voice at me. I could see the devil coming out! I sensed I was in danger!

I decided to stop an incoming taxi and off I went – never allowing my gaze to leave his moves. I could tell he was waiting for the taxi to reach a good distance, before he left and started his journey – thinking that he won the race and got me off his back.

I then realized, though he called me an idiot for all my life. Though he devalued me for all my life. Though he inflicted both physical and emotional pain and trauma to me – It was now time to play my role as a son. Never to pay evil for evil. He needed help and the smart cookie that I turned out to be, will out-smart him.

I stopped the taxi, got off, though I didn't know the area, I believed that most streets were connected to each other if you don't allow yourself to go too far off. So, I beat him to it. I was able to catch up with him and observed where he was heading until he reached his destination.

As I saw where my once financially well-off father lived, I cried till there were no more tears left in my tear ducts. My father, who had owned businesses, who once had a home and a car to care for his five children and wife, who was known in his community for his generosity, was now destitute.

That day, I realized that life is merciless! Worst, when we don't show mercy to our loved ones and to others.

As I stood there, I felt sad! I felt angry! I felt hopeless!

I felt robbed!

As a young man, standing there, a movie was being played in my mind as to what life would have been like if my father had actually been a father to me.

I pictured the interactions and behaviors of my friends whose fathers were very much present in their lives with whom they had a loving and supportive relationship. The movie scene that kept on repeating itself was this:

- The way they socialized was different than I did!

- They seemed to do better in school than I did!

- They seemed to express themselves better than I did!

- They seemed to interact better with other boys than I did!

- They seemed to interact better with girls than I did!

- They seemed to have a path that was forged for them, but I didn't!

- They seemed to be hopeful about the future, but I was hopeless!

- They had someone or a taxi to pick them up from school, but I had none! Depending on where I was living, I had to walk at least 10 km one way to get school.

- They had someone to show up for parent-teachers meetings, but I had none!

- They brought lunch to school or had money to buy lunch, but I had to do odd jobs after school to have lunch money the next day.

- They had everything going for them, but I had everything going against me.

As I was still standing there, profusely crying, and looking at where my father was living. For the life of me, I simply cannot describe my father's living situation out of respect for him.

All I can say is that he was destitute. And all I could see was a path that I didn't want to end up on.

The thoughts kept on resounding in my mind:

> "Why is it that the ones in my circle are known to be the losers in town?"

> "Why is it that the drug dealers won't leave me alone?"

"Why is it that the girls who wanted to hang around with me were the ones who were always preoccupied with sex while I had no interest in that?"

"Why is it that the teachers did not take any interest in me?"

The thoughts were racing and drowning my soul, there I stood and resolved within myself that no one can fix me but me.

My father allowed his past unresolved issues to break him and to drag him down to such a low, pitiful state, I must prove him wrong of everything he said about me.

I will make my late mother proud of the son she left behind at the age of five.

I will make my siblings proud of their little brother whom they poured so much into.

I will not be like my father falling from grace.

I will make a difference – I will make something of myself.

As I looked at my father in the lowest state any human being could be and although he never saw me in my discovery of his makeshift "shelter" made of cardboards in an open field, I asked, deep down in my soul with tears flowing down my face like a torrential rain:

> "Father, how did you allow this to happen to you?"

> "Father, how did you drag your children into this?"

> "Father, how do you expect me to react to you in such a state?"

> "Father, how do you expect me to report your low state of dwelling to my siblings?"

> "Father, how can you expect me to share this story with my children, your grandchildren?

> "Father, how do you expect me to follow in your footsteps.?"

As I was deeply involved in this inner monologue, I was in deep agony with myself. My heart was wrapped with anger, grief, despair, and hopelessness.

"How can I escape this?" I asked!

Then, I looked up to the heaven above where the God of my late mother, Rosana, resides.

The heavenly father whom I thought abandoned me and I said:

> "God, you took my mother away from me before I could count, as of now, please count me among your sons. Help me make something out of myself, for I am a nobody. I don't really know you, but my mother knew you. I have not been to church that often since you took her away from me, please help me for her sake.
>
> Please, take this curse away from me."

Does God Hear Our Cry?

At the time when I uttered those words to God, I really didn't expect Him to hear, much less to reply. After all, I went through so much hardship in the past and I really felt He didn't care.

This seems to be the natural human reaction when going through difficulties. You pray and He seems to be silent.

In my case, it was rather painful to address God as my heavenly father because my earthly father failed me terribly – he was brutal to me therefore such a parallel didn't resonate well with me – worst, He sat on His throne above and watched me endure such pain and suffering.

It took years later for me to reflect on this "prayer" and be able to answer this question, does God hear our cries?

Now, I can confidently say: "Yes, He does!"

My life today is a living proof of the fact that He heard when I cried to Him addressing Him as the God of my mother.

Most of the things I asked Him for, He granted them unto me.

Like David, it didn't happen overnight, it was as the result of hard work, trials and errors, joy, and sorrow. The things He chose not to grant me, I don't know why but I will say like Job,

"Though He slay me, yet will I trust Him…"[2]

Your relationship with God may not be at its best now due to what you are going through. You may be asking Him a lot of questions. It's okay to ask questions, questioning is also a good sign. It means you are interested to know more. You want to know Him better. You want to know His will. You want to know why He allows certain things to happen to you. He won't give up on you – even if you give up on Him. In due season, just like Job and just like me, you will soon see the benefits of trusting Him.

His plan on your life is stamped all over you even when you can't see it. It's recorded in Jeremiah 29:11

> "For I know the plans I have for you, plans to prosper you and not to harm you, plans to give you hope and a future. Then, you will call on Me and come to Me, and I will listen to you."[3]

Don't allow your circumstances to break you but rather to make you.

God didn't promise to take away the waters from under your bridge nor did He promise to extinguish the fire that's raging in your life.

He rather promised in Isaiah 43:2,

"When you pass through the waters, I will be with you; and when you pass through the rivers, they will not sweep over you. When you walk through the fire, you will not be burned; the flames will not set you ablaze."[4]

Don't sit in the water but walk through it. Don't settle in the fire, walk through it for God is with you.

As the apostle Paul puts it in Philippians 4:6-7,

"Do not be anxious about anything, but in every situation, by prayer and petition, with thanksgiving, present your requests to God. And the peace of God, which transcends all understanding, will guard your hearts and your minds in Christ Jesus."[5]

Jennie Allen, writes in her book, *Get Out of Your Head*:

> "God's promises give us ultimate hope in absolutely every circumstance. He meets every need. He will resolve (in the end) every problem we may face here on earth."[6]

Your problems included!

CHAPTER 8
The Unhealed Wounds
of My Father

—.—

"From the womb to the tomb, we will experience the wounds of life, but ... We shall overcome!"

Emile Maxi

—.—

The Second and Final Reunion with My Father

After leaving that place where I was observing my father's dwelling place, I took my long walk back to the main road and took a taxi home. The taxi ride was long as you would have expected. The agonizing thoughts, the non-verbal monologue, the condition of his living situation, I was trying to process all of that. That day was probably one of my saddest days.

When I got home, my eldest sister, Suze, wanted to know why it took me so long. The journey one way was probably about two hours, I really can't tell you for sure. But it was longer due to my spying on my father's dwelling place and the floods of emotions and my internal reflective talks with myself.

I reported it to Suze, and she was in shock! Again, within a matter of days, dad came back to live with us. By this time, my sister Mathurine had already joined back the church – my parents' denominational root; the Seventh-day Adventist Church. Through her influence, I joined the Seventh-day Adventist Church, the church of my childhood and I was baptized.

I gave Bible Studies to my sister Suze and through my influence, she also joined the Seventh-day Adventist Church and was baptized. Then, my elder sister Rosana, also joined the church.

My father was changed but not by much. I shouldn't have expected much because the only way one can experience long, and lasting change is by acknowledging that there is a problem and that something needs to be done to change it.

In this case, my father, with a long history of domestic violence and personal trauma, the only way that he could resolve it, is if he had sought help and was willing to do whatever it took to work on himself so that he could create a better version of himself.

We are never too broken that we can't be mended. We are never too empty that we can't be filled. We are never too traumatized that we can't reset our brain-clock. It is all a matter of personal decision.

If you are really in love with your spouse, love your children and love your loved-ones, when you see them hurting as the result of you, inflicting the hurts on them, you can't be so prideful that you can't disarm yourself of this lethal venom that leaves them emotionally disturbed or paralyzed and to take the initiative to inject the antidote, one that is full of humility accompanied by a sense of remorse for your actions. Apologize, ask for forgiveness, and pursue long and lasting reconciliation.

In his book, *The Art of a Genuine Apology*, Andrew L. Blackwood writes,

> "When someone chooses to apologize, it can be a sign of great strength. People who shy away from accepting responsibility are simultaneously refusing to be

open to growth and are actively shutting down opportunities to bring healing to the people they love, making their relationship weaker. Choosing to acknowledge one's errors and apologize demonstrate that someone is brave enough to acknowledge their imperfections and accept that they have room to grow."[1]

Anyone with a heart that palpitates will be willing to grant forgiveness even when the heart is still hurt and bleeding. That's the nature of mankind. The heart was made to love, it won't be happy until it gives love unreservedly. That's why it hurts so much when the hurt comes from the one who occupies a place in your heart – it bleeds out tears of sorrow.

Have I forgiven my father?

Sure, I have!

Regardless of what happened to you, you can't expect to be emotionally free until you free your mind and your heart of the pain of disappointments and the hurts inflicted on you. This is a commitment that you ought to make to yourself – Commit to forgive, you will experience true freedom.

Failing to forgive will keep you in your own private jail cell and that's detrimental, not just to your mental and emotional health but also your physical health will greatly suffer.

I have forgiven my father, though he never, in the least of a conversation showed any remorse, apologized, asked for forgiveness. I have come to the realization that I needed to forgive him for my own sake and for my own emotional freedom.

As a pastor, I have been at the bed side of lots of terminally ill people who, before they took their last breath, would ask me to gather their family members around them and one by one, they addressed them and made peace before they die. It has always been very humbling to watch.

They would thank me for my ministry, for the act of helping them make peace with their loved-ones and for the fact that they can depart from this world in peace.

This, at least, provides closure for both parties.

In my case, I never had closure with my father. He died suddenly.

The wounds were always fresh, until I decided to heal them myself.

I did what I needed to do to close them, dressing the wounds inflicted on me by my father, so that I can be a better husband, a better father, a better friend, and a better human being!

And I keep working on the other wounds that life keeps on inflicting me, for this is the work of a lifetime.

If the same thing happened to you, I implore you to close your emotional wounds yourself.

It's a choice!

No one can close them for you but you! And it takes a strong mindset!

Don't expect time to heal your wounds – Time heals nothing. It's what you do within the time that heals. Work on yourself!

You can't continue living your life with fresh emotional wounds though inflicted many years ago. By closing them, you will heal your heart. This will be the beginning of a new you and a new world.

Your world can't be new until you are new!

Your relationship with your spouse and your loved ones can't be healed until you heal yourself.

When Calamity Strikes

If we had only stopped to ponder on how short our lifespan is, we would have probably treated each other better. We would show the love. Unfortunately, far too often we wait until one is dead to say all the good things but it's too late.

When our loved ones are gone, our tears at times only reflect the things we wished were said or were never said, the things we wished were done or were never done.

At times we wished we had said more to express our love and admiration for the person while alive – but it's too late. We wished we had shown more compassion, but too late. We wished … and the wishes bleed out tears of sorrow for what could have been – but too late!

In his book, *Life on Purpose*, Victor J. Strecher says this, "Over 2,300 years ago, Aristotle posed one of the most important philosophical questions: What is the ultimate purpose of human activity?"[2]

He concluded "the ultimate purpose of human activity is happiness."[3]

This, I believe my eldest sister Suze understood well. There can be no happiness without dad at home at a time when others are celebrating and at a time when he needed us the most.

My eldest sister insisted that we take back our father to live with us after I reported the condition that I saw him in. As usual, she had become the mother of us all. She was the voice of wisdom and reason, though at that time she was approaching her thirtieth birthday. She had committed her life back to God probably a year or two earlier. Life took a different turn. My dear sister, the one who carried us all on her back, now my father included, she became ill.

If prayer could have brought God down to perform a unique and special miracle, the prayers of the Hebron Seventh-day Adventist Church in Delmas, Port-Au-Prince, Haiti, would have done just that.

Through her illness, everyone became extremely united to do whatever was necessary to care for the almost thirty-year old beautiful soul who blessed humanity with her presence.

Through the presence of my devoted and beautiful sister and godmother, Suze Maxi, I have come to believe that the Almighty God created each one of us for a purpose and with a shelf life. Once we have fulfilled that purpose, our shelf life comes to expiration – it's time to depart this world.

In this case, my eldest sister Suze, after she faithfully took the place of our mother, she saw us all turning adults and my father back home, she succumbed to her illness and never recovered. She died on her birthday – at the age of thirty years old, living in our care, two beautiful girls who were just as young as I was when my mother died.

The day Suze died; was the day my father started his slow journey to his grave. I remembered him, saying: "you guys can now prepare for my funeral – now Suze is gone, there is no reason for me to live. Life is not worth living. Suze was the apple of my eye."

I didn't mind hearing him say that – I knew it all my life. She was such a beautiful soul, I was glad that my father, in all his brokenness, his heart was filled with love for his eldest daughter that we all loved and admired. Unfortunately, he didn't show it. He didn't know how to show it. He was never cultured to show love and affection, but his heart was still broken!

On the day of my eldest sister's funeral, my father looked lost and bewildered. Lost in all hope of having his beloved first born around him. From that moment on, he never took any pleasure in life but rather looked forward to the day when he would depart this world and put an end to a heart full of pain and suffering due to the hard blows that life inflicted on him from his childhood - the death of my mother and now the death of his first born.

One afternoon, I came home from sitting my high school exit exam, he died seven months after the death of my eldest sister Suze. At this time, many of us finished high school later due to political coups and civil unrest. I was twenty-one years old; my heart was still full of pain and anxiety from the loss of my beloved sister who cared for me since I was five years old following the death of my mother. My father's heart was filled with previous unhealed wounds and now freshly inflicted wounds brought on him by the death of his favorite child which he said many times over, he couldn't recuperate from this loss.

That evening, I came home, I found him writhing in agony and short of breath. My brother and I chartered a taxi, we put him to sit in the middle to ensure that our bodies would support him from collapsing on the seat. He leaned towards me, rest his head on my left shoulder, the one to whom he inflicted the most emotional blows, and to ensure his comfort, I put his head to rest on my lap, there he took his last breath and died — inflicting on me the final deadly blow that scared me forever.

The lap that used to be the seat of his merciless lashes, became his resting place at death! The son of sorrow became the son of comfort! Nonetheless, I am glad he had my lap to lean on at death!

At his burial, a friend of the family who knew what I went through, came, stood by me, then put his hand around my shoulders and said to me:

"Now that your father is gone, no more beatings. You can now live a happy life. Rejoice my son, rejoice. It's all over!"

As the casket was going into the vault for the burial, my mind started racing as to what life would have been if I had a father who cared. A father who loved, a father who modeled, a father who would have prepared me to be a good husband and a good father.

I was staring at the casket with a myriad of questions for which I had no answers.

I didn't cry for the death of my father because all the tears that were in my tear ducts had already gushed the streams of pain and suffering of yester years. Though I didn't cry, the pains of emotional abuse, physical abuse, psychological abuse and passed on trauma were sitting on my chest like the weight of a dead elephant. It was heavy!

Respect Due

As a son, I paid my respect to the man, both in life and in death. I never once disrespected him, but I was there at his graveside hoping that he had played his role as a real father to a son. Hoping that we had a relationship. Hoping that he had shown me how to be a man, a good citizen and the list goes on. My wish list was so long but the man was dead, therefore, there is no need to wish for anything as that chapter was now closed. I was so lost in my thoughts – grieving the death of my sister, Suze seven months prior and now my father's death.

The Decision to Migrate to Jamaica

The day I left the burial ground of my father, was the day I decided that I would leave Haiti. I loved and admired my remaining siblings, they did so much for me. If it were not for them, I don't think I would be here today to write a book. But the pain of my heart was by far too heavy to continue living in my country of birth.

Life without my eldest sister, Suze was becoming unbearable. The sight of seeing such a young lady dying from the illness that took her life at the age of twenty-nine – turning thirty on the day she passed away, her birthday, August 23, 1987. I couldn't muster up the courage to see my siblings suffer.

What broke the camel's back was that, by this time, the political and economic landscape of Haiti had gone down to the ditch therefore, any young person who had a dream for the future and could flee, must flee by whatever safe and proper means. It's funny how someone can love his or her country even though it is known as a poor and unsafe place.

Although I have left Haiti since August of 1988, I have been back only twice, the last time was in 1997. Regardless of what's going on in my poor country, I still love it and have fond memories of it which I will cherish for the rest of my life.

Life is full of odds!

Within seven months, I had to deal with two deaths:

The death of my eldest sister Suze, who poured into me the most love any child could ask for!

The death of my father who inflicted in me the most pain any child should run away from!

I was grieving the loss of someone who built me, and I was grieving the loss of someone who destroyed me!

I was broken from both ends!

CHAPTER 9
We Shall Overcome

—·—

*"No wounds can be healed
until the desire to heal the pain
is greater."*

Emile Maxi

—·—

In her book, *Rising Strong*, Brené Brown says, "We are the authors of our lives. We write our own daring endings."[1]

This is so true!

There is a probability that reading this book causes you as much pain as it did me, reliving my ordeal experience in the process of writing it. I have given you a lot of headaches by putting this hard and graphic stuff in a book for you to read. Believe me, it takes everything from me to share this with you. This is the very first time I have shared this painful experience. Everything in me ached in the process of writing it! It's like it was yesterday.

Why am I sharing this hard stuff with you?

I do so for several reasons:

1. I want you to understand that you are not alone. In those days, I used to think that I was alone in my pain and suffering. I even used to think that God had turned His back on me. If I am to be honest with you, even now, when I think of the pain and suffering of innocent people, I ask the question: "God, where are you?"

   Indeed, at times, God's silence can be deafening! That was the cry of the prophet Habakkuk!

I want to remind you that God remains at the same place where He was when His son, Jesus Christ was dying on the cross!

At times, when God seems to be far, guess who moved? I moved! You moved!

You may be asking the same question or saying the same things. We may be different, but our pain is the same. This leads me to the next point.

2. Talking or writing is therapeutic. In fact, why do you think, according to scientific evidence, women live longer than men? Women are not afraid to talk about their problems. Men are! They don't want to appear weak. They believe they can solve their own problems even if they are dying. That's a false impression of strength. As men, we were trained on falsehood. If you have ever gone for counselling, you would now understand why you do most of the talking while the counsellor or the therapist does most of the listening. According to statistics, men are more susceptible to die of a heart attack than women, simply because men bottle things up and suffer in silence. For a long time, I would never talk about these things, although they were the root cause of my nightmare episodes, which caused me a lot of anxiety.

Now, I can talk about it. Better yet, I can write about it so that it can help someone like you. Similarly, if you want to heal yourself from your past emotional pain and trauma, you will need to deal with it head-on. Don't just keep complaining about what happened – Seek professional help. Be intentional about dealing with the issue. This will be the beginning of your healing process.

3. I want you to understand that the odds are real. Embrace the reality of the odds. Let the odds work for you, not against you. Allow them to build you, not destroy you. Let them give you a sense of self determination to take full responsibility for your healing and for your success. Never allow your past, present or future disappointments define who you really are.

This does not mean that the odds, the trauma, or the bad experiences will not come back as a ghost to haunt you, but you must resolve in yourself that you are the sole architect and engineer of your life.

Take your broken pieces, put them together and reconstruct yourself, just as the Japanese craftsman repairs a broken vessel, after all, no one can do it for you but you!

Some years ago, if you had told me that I would become who I am today, I would have told you that it's impossible based on how low I was in life. To be where I am now is because of hard work, professional help and reading a lot of self-help books on emotional health. I went through many grief recovery sessions to address the unresolved issues in my life as I have shared with you so far and to ensure that I am not simply living but I am thriving.

As a Grief Recovery Specialist, I am devoted to helping others take care of their emotional health so that they too, can have the peace that I now have.

I now have an inner peace that I can't explain. This is my wish for you! On a few occasions, while waiting patiently in line in a store, for instance, someone would come to me and ask:

"Sir, do you mind if I ask you a question?"

"Sure", I would reply with a smile!

Then, the person would say, "I have been observing you for a few minutes, you are so calm. So peaceful, we can't even explain how calm you are. Anything in particular...that causes you to be so calm?"

I would smile and reply: "I do feel at peace indeed! My heart is so light, I must admit, I can't even explain it myself ... All I know is that I work on myself daily to develop this sense of peace..."

On one occasion, my reply to someone was: "When I look in the rear-view mirror, I see where I am coming from, for me it was painful. So, I won't go back. I keep moving forward by looking through the windshield. The past is there only to remind me of the pain I went through to reach this point. It is too painful to carry on my journey which I intend to enjoy. Therefore, I focus on my personal sense of happiness and the happiness of others which give me a sense of peace that I can't explain…"

To have that peace, it requires hard and intentional work on "self."

Depending on the weight of your emotional baggage, you can't work on it by yourself, you may need help! I have been doing pre and post marital counselling, grief recovery support and life coaching for a while now, unfortunately, men are the last to admit that they need help, even when they are on the verge of losing their wives or their children. This, to me, is very sad!

Always remember this; "It takes strength to stand alone but it takes wisdom to seek help and to lean on others."

I would like for you to understand that the state of your inner peace is not the absence of chaos in your external world but rather your ability to control it from the inside. You can't control what happened to you, but you can control how you allow it to affect you.

I have worked hard on myself to achieve this peace! So can you!

I have worked hard to achieve great things despite the odds! You too can!

To soar against the odds, you must accept the odds for what they are worth but never allow them to define who you are. Don't try to fix your odds! Try to fix yourself!

It will not be easy, but it is possible! If I can do it! So can you!

Yes, I know! The things that happened to you left you some emotional, psychological, and inter-generational scars that are so deep that it transcends all human understanding, and you might be saying: "It's easier said than done, because he who feels it, knows it."

I can appreciate that, but, let me tell you, your hurt, hurts us all. It hurts your spouse. It hurts your children. They are not only hurting by watching you being hurt, but you are also hurting them by your words and actions unfortunately. By doing this, you are inflicting more emotional pain to them that will scar them for life, hence inter-generational trauma. If you really love them, do your part to stop passing it on!

Not only does it hurt your immediate family, but it also hurts your loved ones and your friends. It can even hurt anyone who has had an encounter with you.

As the saying goes "hurt people hurt people." That's why there's so much hurt in the world today. We are all carrying some unresolved emotional issues and we fail to deal with them.

Our wounds won't be healed until the desire to heal the pain is greater than the pain of the wound itself.

From the womb to the tomb, we will experience the wounds from our odds in life, but regardless of it all, we shall overcome!

The songs which we now know as negro spirituals were songs sung by the African American slaves as a way of appeasing their soul to find hope in the face of hopelessness. They found internal peace in the face of external chaos, finding strength where weakness would have been a reasonable act of acceptance of the odds of life. Their bodies were in chains, but their minds were in the pursuit of freedom hence, hope was born! Even in bondage, the human mind can still dream big dreams of mental and emotional freedom – after all, freedom begins in the mind!

How can I overcome the odds of life; you ask? You will overcome them only through an undeniable awareness that there is a problem, the will to solve it, the determination to do everything in your power to address it, and the right attitude to propel you to pass into action now with the help of meaningful people.

Resolve in yourself that you will make a difference. To make a difference, you need to be different.

Lessons From My Wilderness Experience

Never underestimate nor neglect the valuable lessons of your wilderness experience. There, you are shaped to withstand the test of time. Your successes and your failures are all determined during that time.

You must arm yourself with the will to succeed and the right attitude to soar while in your wilderness. If you do, the bad experiences will be your stepping-stones to success for you would have gained a heart of resilience and self-discipline. Then, nothing can stop you!

You will realize that:

- You can never be too broken that you can't be mended.

- You can never be too bound that you can't be free.

- You can never be too sick that you can't be healed.

- You can never be too poor that you can't be rich.

- You can never be too small that you can't become great.

It all depends on you!

Whatever odds life gives you; you are encouraged to take responsibility as to how you will allow them to affect you.

This is one of the most important lessons we emphasize in grief recovery sessions. This is your first and most important step towards emotional health.

We have all been through our wilderness experiences. Not all of us learned from them! Often, we fail to accept the fact that these heartbreaking crucibles are our greatest teachers. Regardless of how bad they were, they shape us into who we are now or who we will be in the future. We should use them to our advantage.

A knife in the hand of an ill-intentioned person can harm. However, a knife in the hand of a surgeon can heal.

Imagine that this knife is now in your hand - you determine what role you play!

The odds of life can be that knife. It is in your hand. Don't let it harm you. Use it to heal you so that you can be the best version of yourself!

Use it to surgically remove the emotional tumors before they turn out to be an emotional cancer that affect the quality of your life or might even take your life away.

To illustrate this, I will use a character in the Bible that helped me during my struggles as I studied his life. I won't cover everything about him, but I will draw some lessons from his life. If you are not a person of faith, please don't allow my quoting the Bible to cause you to put down this book.

His name is David, his life is recorded in 1 Samuel 16 through to 2 Samuel 24 and 1 King 1-2.

David is one of the patriarchs in the Old Testament of the Bible. In fact, if you are not too familiar with Bible characters, let me remind you that Abraham, Moses, and David constitute the foundational pillars of the Jewish nation. The New Testament writers, even Jesus Christ referred to him numerous times.

Jesus was referred to as the son of David, according to Matthew 1:1-17 and Mark 10:47.

The Odds Are Inevitable

As you recall, earlier, I defined the odds as "the probability that whatever we had planned for or had hoped for may not turn out to be the way we had thought of, planned for, or anticipated."

Towards the end of the reign of Saul, the first king of Israel, it is recorded in 1 Samuel 15:35. "…and the Lord regretted that He had made Saul king over Israel."

Can you imagine God, regretting having done something?

To mitigate for this regret, He sent Samuel in search for a king to replace Saul. God was in search of someone who could work with Him even when the odds were against him.

That person was David!

He was not the first born of his parents - he was the youngest child. His place was in the fields to take care of his father's sheep. He was to be seen and not heard. So much so that when the prophet Samuel showed up after receiving divine instructions to go to the house of Jesse the Bethlehemite, this young lad's name was not even mentioned. No one would ever fathom that it was going to be the one whose dwelling place was in the wilderness caring for his father's sheep.

As a matter of fact, in preparation for the sacrifice, and the anointing, the prophet sanctified the seven sons of Jesse. This suggests that David was not part of this at all for he was away in the wilderness taking care of the sheep.

The prophet Samuel himself, when presented with the sons of Jesse, was convinced the Lord had chosen Eliab, the tall and handsome son, to be the next king! One by one they passed before him but surprisingly, none of the seven sons of Jesse presented to the prophet to be examined, were considered for the highest office in the land.

The most interesting part of it all is that the one that God had His eyes on was not even thought of, let alone sanctified to have the right to participate in the sacrifice.

Where was the eighth son? He was in the wilderness taking care of sheep. He was too little and too young to be considered. He didn't have much going for him as far as their plans were concerned yet, unbeknown to him, he had everything going for him because the eyes of the Almighty God were on him.

What does it say to you?

There are times when, as the result of some circumstances of life, you don't weigh much in the scale of others. Whether it is as the result of your lack of education, your social or ethnic background, an illness, your financial status, there is One who, despite your bad circumstances, who is endowed with divine discernment, who sees in you what others can't see.

Those who can't see that in you, should not be blamed!

All it means is that they just don't have the expertise to see diamond in the rough. To see the leader in the making! To see the broken that's about to be mended! To see the bound that's about to be let loose!

That diamond is you!

You may not have any hope for the future, right now, but remember, the eyes of the Almighty God are on you.

Do you recall the prayer I prayed to God when I stood there and saw where my father was living. The time when I cried to the God of my deceased mother to count me among His sons!

Let me tell you, our God isn't deaf. He is very attentive to every word that comes out of our mouth.

Make no mistake about this, if at times He seems to be far away, guess who moved? It was you or I who moved, not Him!

He has already provided everything for you to reach your full potential. It might be dormant in the cradle of your mind, but it is there, and it is possible.

You need to reach out for it. He wants you to work hard for it so that you can better appreciate it.

Why?

Because He knows, "Whatever is appreciated, appreciates."

Whatever He has in store for you will not come by wishing and hoping. It will come as the direct result of working hard and smart for it, and by having the right people in your life.

For David, it was Samuel and later Jonathan!

For me, it was my siblings: Suze, Rosana, Ascencio and Mathurine, my aunts, my uncles, my cousins, my kind-hearted neighbours and later, my church family and my dear friend Jean Claude Dorval.

Who is it for you?

You may not have been counted among the ones with great potential because of your low state, low self-esteem, lack of education or humble beginning, but I am here to tell you that the fact your father, your mother or your caregiver didn't place value on you doesn't mean that you are not valuable.

You should not allow your circumstances to determine your self-worth. You might be down in the mud as the result of what you went through, but I am encouraging you to find that self-worth from within.

You are valuable! This value is placed upon you by the One who created you – The Almighty God.

If you were to take a one-hundred-dollar bill, crush it and cast it to the dirt, the fact that it's crushed and covered in dirt, doesn't devalue its worth. It remains a one-hundred-dollar bill. Similarly, you may be crushed, and in the dirt of your circumstances, but that doesn't devalue you. You are still valuable!

Learning In Tough Times

In the case of David, because of his birth position, his job was in the wilderness, taking care of his father's sheep. While doing so he made it his point of duty not to take his anger on the animals, but rather to learn in the process. After all, the animals had nothing to do with where he landed!

When life throws us in the wilderness of despair, let's not take it out on the ones under our care. We need to learn valuable lessons that will make us better!

What did David learn in the process?

Let me suggest to you a few of the things that I believe he learned in the wilderness:

- *Patience.* As they say, patience is a virtue but most of us can't stand it. Whatever we desire, we want it now. When we have no control over the situation and we must wait, we murmur. We become anxious. We fail to accept the fact that the lessons we learn from the process of waiting for the purpose of God in our life provides us with virtue. Here, waiting doesn't mean to sit and do nothing. Neither does it mean you must pray and do nothing or leave it to God. You must put action behind your prayer, and something will come out of it.

- *Wisdom.* One of the things we can learn when the odds are against us is wisdom. Unfortunately, all of us want to be wise but not all of us are willing to pay the price to obtain wisdom. For we now know that failures, mistakes, and disappointments are the price we pay to obtain wisdom. For David, while in the wilderness tending his father's sheep, he had to learn from his mistakes to know when to speak and when to be quiet. When to act and when to retreat. This he had to develop so that he could protect his sheep and himself from the elements of nature. If we are going to soar, this is one of the very important attributes we need. You may be frustrated about your current situation now but soon; you will appreciate the hard lessons you had to learn which made you now a wiser person – a person of insight. When the hard times come, take them with a smile. Open your mind to learn as much as you can during your wilderness experience. Very soon, others will benefit from your wise counsels.

- *Innovation.* In the absence of the real and the tangible, we are forced to find alternatives to supply our needs. Every single modern innovation came as the result of someone trying to explore new ideas to improve on their quality of life or developing something that becomes rather indispensable to us today.

  - For the Wright brothers, it was an airplane.

  - For Thomas Edison, it was the incandescent light bulb.

- For the printer, it was Johannes Gutenberg

- For the Computer, it was Charles Baggage

For David, it was a sling shot which was his weapon of defense to keep predators from preying on his father's sheep. When attacked by the big mammals, he rescued his sheep from the lions and the bears by using his bare hands to tear apart the jaws of these big creatures to save his flock.

This mindset and these rare abilities imposed on him by tough times were very useful for him to take down the strong and the mighty that saved and built the nation of Israel.

Similarly, the rough edges of life's crucibles prepare us for tougher times ahead.

David was never perceived as a king, not even by his own father, yet there was something in him that God saw - his character.

While you are in your wilderness, allow whatever comes your way to help you in your character development. Just as the positive and the negative poles of the battery that powers up your vehicle, it is the good and the bad things of life that will power who you are. You decide how they affect you!

Make use of every situation, good or bad!

Be patient!

Be innovative!

Be hopeful!

Be resilient!

Be compassionate!

Be respectful!

Be positive!

Be wise!

Predispose yourself to be a constant learner, regardless of your age.

Waste no time complaining! You may not have the right tool but use what you have.

During the years when my siblings and I were separated, I had nothing! While, I was living with my uncle-in-law, he was hardly home. Most of the time I had nothing to eat. I had to learn to use what I had. My shoe-shining skills!

When we all lived with our father, this was one of my house chores. My father couldn't stand to see dirty shoes. My responsibility was to clean them. At least three times a week, it was a long line of shoes to clean. I used to hate it, but I had no choice. Every single pair had to be shiny that my dad could see his face on the glow of the shoeshine.

I had to use three different cleaning products to ensure that the shoes shined. If not, I would have to do it all over again. To avoid that, I had to take my time to ensure that every single pair of shoes was spotless.

My father valued cleanliness. Our hair had to be well combed, our shirts had to be well tucked in our pants, and our shoes must be always shiny. We always had to be neatly dressed!

Even when I was hungry to the point of fainting, I was always well dressed, my black hair well combed – a trait that dad taught us, that became second nature to me even today!

People wondered how an eleven-year-old boy, tall and thin, could keep himself so spick and span, prim and proper, even in the face of poverty.

During my years of living with my uncle-in-law, he felt it was not his responsibility to provide me with anything more than a roof over my head. He never offered me food. After all, he was hardly home, so having to provide for myself at such young age, I used the only thing that I knew how, shining shoes! No one could beat me at that!

That became my means of income for either cash or food!

My shoes, oh gosh! Always clean even on dusty roads! I carried my little shoe cleaning cloth to ensure that no particle of dust could last on my shiny shoes. Everyone in my neighbourhood wanted me to clean their shoes so theirs could look like mine. They wanted to know the secret, but that was *my* secret commodity. That was my trademark.

"I will do it for you at a cost, but I can't tell you the exact product I use. That's only for me, but I will trade service for cash or for food." I used to tell them.

Soon, I became the man! Well, back then, the shoe-shine boy. The best!

Where did I learn that? In the wilderness of despair! In the end, the very thing I used to hate, now became my source of income. Similarly, regardless how tough life might be for you, use it to your advantage. Be innovative!

You may not like the brutality of life, but never underestimate the valuable lessons of your small and humble beginning! Make good use of your wilderness experience! It wasn't meant to break you but to make you.

Change Your Attitude, Change Your World.

Our world won't change until we develop an attitude of gratitude.

If you were to do a search in the dictionary for the word "disappointment," words such as these would come up as the synonyms:

- Displeasure

- Distress

- Discontent

- Disenchantment

- Disillusion

- Frustration

- Regret

However, if you were to do a search in the dictionary for the antonym, let's use "bliss," words such as these would come up:

- Ecstasy

- Enjoyment

- Delight

- Pleasure

- Harmony

- Blissfulness

To what degree has your life been filled with any of the above, either the synonym or the antonym, disappointments, or blissfulness?

Who in this life does not have his or her own fair share of these two opposite words?

You may be saying, "well, some have it worse than others…!

Yes, I agree with you, some have it worse than others.

But what really makes the difference?

Is it the disappointments or the blissfulness?

Or

Is it our attitude?

This is what I really want you to change - Your attitude to either of the two. Your blissfulness can change at the snap of a finger. No one could have told my father that there was a possibility for him to lose his wealth. However, when he did lose it, he didn't have the attitude to be resilient enough to make it back, therefore he went into depression and took his anger out on us. We became the victims of his loss.

Similarly, when life's disappointment strikes, even when we lose it all, we need to have the right attitude to know that "a setback, is a setup for a comeback".

The saddest part of failing is not the failure but failing to learn from it.

Reflecting on the Crucibles of Life

What makes you who you are today? The good times or the bad times? Or is it a bit of both? While some may say it's both, personally, I believe that the misfortunes of life have a more positive impact on us in terms of shaping us for future challenges. If we learned well from the misfortunes of life, we could turn them into great fortunes. Very often, life serves us our fortunes on a platter of misfortunes, and we often fail to see it for what it's worth.

Far too often, we find ourselves in the field of life filled with dirt-covered-gold, but our gaze is so focused on the dirt that we become discouraged. We are unable to see the gold inside the dirt and its golden opportunities, and we walk away empty handed. It leaves us in a state of despair and casting blame. We become angry with life and when we speak, we spew out venom, poisoning our loved ones with our words and actions.

We fail to realize that the only person who will be caught and will eventually fall victim in this blame, is the person casting the blame. If we could only accept the reality of life and take full responsibility to transform our disadvantage into our advantage, our misfortune into our fortune, then we would be better off.

In this process, one of the things we need to work on is our character. The oxford dictionary defines it as: "the mental and moral qualities distinctive to an individual." Using this definition, I want to believe that all the things, good or bad, that are happening in our world today hangs on the balance of character.

Our character shapes our personality. Our personality determines our behaviours and our actions, so, what are the things that shape our character?

Our home education - upbringing

Our academic education

Our environment

How we allow these three elements that mold us, to shape our lives and guide our actions is of paramount importance. These are the things that make us into who we are. Their influence on us not only cause us to respond positively or negatively to life but can also determine how we treat each other.

Our Adversity, Our Training Ground

Our best song will be written during our most trying moment. Our best piece of music will be composed during our darkest times. Our best poem will be written during our moment of hopelessness and grief – if we develop the right attitude.

If you were to do a search for the history of some of the most heart-warming songs, you will find that they were composed at the darkest moment in the life of the composers. This proves to be true for most of the songs you hear whether they are gospel or not.

As human beings, we express our emotions through words. When they too become overwhelming, we express them through the shedding of tears, though at times through anger and or through withdrawals, of which the latter are the most concerning ways of expressing our emotions – the last two can be lethal.

If we can sing, we write songs. If we can play an instrument, we write music. If we can write poems, we do poetry. If we like writing, we journal or we write books. These are healthy ways to express our emotions.

If you write songs, poetry, or books, those who will be exposed to your work and to your method of communicating the dark moments of life, will relate to your sorrow and your pain. If the message you communicate is done with positivity or as a cry for help, they will find strength in your weakness. They will find light through your darkness. They will find hope through your hopelessness. Hence, their spirit will be lifted. This can be an effective means to provide healing to the broken heart.

As a Grief Recovery Specialist, whenever I do grief recovery support sessions with someone who is severely grieving the loss of any kind, I always encourage them to be mindful of those around them who might be in the same situation. They need to be engaged in a cause that will uplift them instead of pulling them down. They need to provide hope to others though they may experience hopelessness for it is in giving hope that we become hopeful. It is in blessing others that we become blessed – especially in times of adversity.

Similarly, when I do life coaching sessions with individuals, if the person is down and confused about life and their future, I always encourage them to stay far away from people who are pessimistic and negative.

If you are seriously grieving the loss of any kind, the best way to lift yourself up is not to stay among other grievers who use grief as a comfort but rather find others who, though, they, themselves might be experiencing some kind of grief can help lift your spirit. The more you stay among the grievers who like to stay in a state of grief, the more you will grieve. I find that, unresolved grief often leads to depression. If for any reason, you must be among other grievers, you must arm yourself with internal fortitude, focus, clarity of mind, a positive attitude, and the will to help them to bring closure to their state of grief – This can be the work of a long time, depending on the relationship they must work on.

If well accompanied through their grief, the day will come when they will be able to sing songs of hope and comfort. They too will become a blessing to others. A source of encouragement to the discouraged.

The songs that we now know as Negro Spirituals are deep and meaningful.

The slaves found inner strength to compose and to sing songs that were impossible to be understood by someone who did not have that internal resilience and mindset to sing about hope where there seemingly was none in the horizon, yet they saw it.

The words of their songs were their way of encouraging themselves to see what their slave masters could not have seen. Though in chains, the words of their songs freed their minds in a way no slave master could understand.

This allowed them to see what could not have been perceived, it drove them to hope for the unfathomable, it permitted them to endure the unimaginable because they saw something that only those with that mindset could have seen.

Today, when we hear or sing the Negro Spirituals, at times we cry. Why? Because they hit a chord in our soul!

How do you express your sorrow?

I can tell you that during the days when I was living in my dad's house, especially when he sent me to live with my uncle in-law, I was always afraid to show emotions whether that was to laugh or to cry because either of them would get me in trouble. There were days when, sitting quietly and playing by myself would result in some hard kicks to my behind, ribs, or gut.

There were days when I would remember the pleasant times with my siblings and the jokes we used to share, so, I would laugh or smile. He wanted to know what I was laughing or smiling about so he could give me a reason to cry.

If I cry as the result of his slaps on my face, lashes on my back, he would deem that it wasn't hard enough to cause me to cry and would demand that I take off my clothes so that my skin can be well exposed and beat me to the point of inflicting flesh wounds. He would then mix salt in water and pour it into my open wounds causing me to scream for my mother to come for me so that I could rest with her in her grave and escape this brutal hell.

To ensure that I don't attract violence on my skinny self, I learned to express myself internally. I would speak to myself without uttering a word. I was like a crazy person who would talk to himself and laugh or get upset with himself, except in my case, no one knew it, it was all internal.

There were days when singing in the private chamber of my heart was the only thing I had to rely on. Like the slaves, they allowed me to have hope therefore to accept the unacceptable while planning my escape in my mind.

In those days, in the deepest part of my soul, I cried without shedding tears to save myself from unnecessary and unwanted beatings yet, my heart would be filled with sorrow waiting for the tears to explode in a river of tearful, torrential, and painful emotions. A song in my heart always calmed the pain!

This wilderness experience gave birth to something that would help develop a coping mechanism in me - the ability to read any piece of literature I could put my hands on, exercise my cognitive ability to commit to memory whatever I had read so that I could have something to fill my mind to help me think about and to fall asleep at night instead of always thinking of the pain which often drove me into despair.

Then, I started to write as a way of expressing myself. This became very therapeutic for me. That was my way of venting my sadness, concerns, my sense of hopelessness and at times, I even wrote to God because He didn't seem to notice my faint voice, crying for help.

Considering my circumstances then, the skills that I learned earlier in life to help me cope with my odds, and the house duties imposed on me by my dad, were preparing me for something. I did not know those odds were going to work in my favour and helped me to be the best at what I was doing at the age of eleven.

As I reflect on the past, and I want to believe it is the same for you, life's experiences were brutal but, these experiences help to shape us for the unknown. The way we perform our duties now reflects what we learned from past experiences and how we allow them to contribute to our lives.

Today, people complement me for the way my shoes are always clean and sparkling. Those who come by my home, would comment that my lawn is always well manicured. It all comes from my wilderness experience. Though my house was always felt like a bootcamp, I learned something from my father which I am very grateful for; the notion of, "whatever you do, do it to the best of your ability." This remains with me until today.

There are times we will despise the wilderness experience, but they are necessary to our survival. Apply yourself well, learn well, be the best, give your best and it will put you above the rest.

The Irony of Life

As I read 1 Samuel 16:13, I sensed that when the prophet Samuel saw David, the eighth and youngest son of Jesse who was not part of the show as shared with you earlier, he breathed a sigh of relief, "ah, this is the one that God wants me to anoint as King to replace Saul." , so, David was anointed in the presence of his brothers to be the next King of Israel.

The way the story unfolds is rather very interesting. The fact that he was not serving in the army suggests that he was under-age, anywhere between sixteen and nineteen - The permissible age prescribed to be enrolled in the army was age twenty, according to Numbers 1:45.

Yet, he was anointed king in his teenage years, but according to 1 Chronicles 11:1-3 he did not become king until he was thirty. That's between eleven to fourteen years in waiting to take on the throne.

In as much as we would want to believe that this must have been kept top secret, such a thing could not have stayed in secret for too long – after all, they all knew the prophet had anointed him for something special.

My friend, you may not see it yet, but let me tell you that God has anointed you for something, in due time, it will all materialize just work with Him.

We are told that eventually, David got to serve King Saul in the palace.

What really got him there? Was it his anointing? No! At least not yet!

What was it then, that got him there? It was his ability to play the musical instrument called the harp.

David could play it to perfection! He was very skillful at it! Therefore, he was considered for this noble position because of his skillful ability to play and to calm the soul of the disturbed and distressed King Saul.

What can we learn from this?

I would want to believe that David learned to play this instrument to perfection as part of keeping himself from boredom as he cared for his father's sheep in the wilderness.

He learned to adopt and to adapt to his odds because in the university of life, we often gain the experience before we are taught the lesson.

Read this part very carefully. Let it sink in your mind. Here it is, my friend:

He knew why he was anointed but he was prepared to serve before he is served.

This is a lesson of servant leadership that you and I need to learn.

Similarly, you have been anointed for a special task on this planet, don't force your way. Don't despise others. Soar gracefully against the odds. It will be yours in due course. In the meantime, whatever you are asked to do, do it to the best of your ability. Don't shortchange yourself. Don't shortchange others either.

If you are a faithful servant, when you rise to a leadership role, you will better understand the ones placed under your authority, you will be better able to exercise effective leadership because you were once a servant therefore, you will understand the needs of your servants better.

If you allow yourself to have this "servant-leader" attitude, you will see your role at the top as one to help those at the bottom accomplish their dreams and aspirations. This way, you would have fulfilled your duty.

Failing to act based on an attitude of a servant-leader, you would have failed to honour your God-given role and responsibility and why you should be kept at the top of the ladder of leadership. The ladder is there, not just for you to climb on, but for you to take others with you.

You are anointed for something great but don't spoil the show. Allow your wilderness experience to prepare you for what's ahead.

- Don't be so focused on the position that you fail to develop the leader within – That's self-preparation!

- Don't be so passionate to lead that you fail to neglect the ones you are called to lead – That's compassion!

- Don't be so eager to show up for the appointment that you forget to prepare for it – That's personal growth and development!

- Don't be so passionate about the message that you fail to care for the messenger – That's self-care!

- Don't be so confident about the recital that you forget to practice for it – That's keeping yourself on the cutting edge!

- Don't be so fast to reach your destination that you neglect to obey the instructions of your internal GPS – That's your emotional health!

The shepherd boy, though a teenager, he was wise enough to know that he had to wait patiently for his time.

While awaiting, he had to cooperate through the process, he gave his best lest he ruined his chances of succeeding Saul as King of Israel – for which he was anointed!

Similarly, you are called to be faithful to the call of duty even if you must wait much longer than expected. Even when you are mistreated in the process, you are called to be faithful not successful. Once you are, leave "success" to the law of nature that the Almighty God has set over you.

CHAPTER 10
There Is Hope for You

—·—

"It is hopelessly hopeless to be without hope."

Emile Maxi

—·—

Evaluate Your Horizon

We all live under the same sky, but we don't see the same horizon.

Why is it that someone may go through hardship and is crushed under it while someone else who went through either the same thing or even worst withstands its pressure?

When I look back at where I am coming from, I can say that my life was made of crucibles. At that time, I had no choice. Whether it was the time when

I lived in the bootcamp at my father's house, having to experience and endure brutal physical and mental anguish or it was at the time when he placed me to live with my uncle in-law or when I was reunited with my siblings as teenagers, we had to make ends meet even when there were no ends.

I had to accept the fact that life was extremely difficult. In fact, life has never been easy for me.

As bad as it was, I must admit that today, when I look at life and how hard it was, I am grateful for the resilient attitude I developed through my past hardship. If I could survive my past, I can handle anything!

This statement also goes for you!

Don't you ever underestimate the power you have within you.

You are as tough as steal!

You won't know it until you are put to the test.

The way you allow your past crucibles to shape you will allow you to go through the worst and find the inner strength to stand strong knowing that you will come out:

> stronger not weaker,

better not bitter,

armed not harmed.

Prepared for anything life will throw at you. Because of your mental fortitude, others will rely on you for strength, hope and encouragement.

The only way you can be able to offer a helping hand to someone in need is because you went through life's grinder before them, and you made it out:

- bruised but not crushed,

- chipped but not broken,

- knocked down but not knocked out,

- affected but not defeated,

- perplexed but not in despair.

If you are prepared to do certain things differently, you will make it. You can't continue to do the same things repeatedly and expect different results.

This is why I wrote this book. As a Grief Recovery Specialist and Life Coach, that's what I do, help people address the things that need to be addressed in their lives so that they can allow nothing to clip their wings and prevent them from soaring. You were made to soar – So, soar against the odds!

If you had asked me some thirty-five or forty-years ago that I would be writing books one day, I would have told you to schedule an appointment to see a psychiatrist. Based on the landscape of things, my future then was not just deemed, it was hopeless, but, through it all, I knew there must have been something better somewhere.

The Power of Positive People and Positive Words

My external wilderness was rather arid, but my internal wilderness was very much a fertile soil, watered by a spring of possibilities that was filled with dreams and aspirations.

These dreams and aspirations were nurtured by my resilience, by my siblings who assisted me though we were all in the same boat, and by friends who breathed life into me – saying things that I didn't know I could become.

The Jonathan Who Will Love You Unconditionally

I recalled when I was between the ages of fifteen and twenty, I had found such a friend. His name is Jean Claude Dorval. We are still friends after more than forty years.

In those days, I had nothing to offer to anyone. This is the best time to know if a friend is indeed true. Jean Claude lived in a nice upscale area. He didn't have to work to send himself to school. He was active and popular at church. His mother and other relatives were living in the USA and sending money to take care of him. He played the guitar and the piano. He was smart! I had none of these things. Yet, being two young men and committed Christians, we became like brothers.

There were days, if I didn't have anything to eat, I would go to his house and I would have something to eat. When his mother sent him money from the USA, he would give me some money so that I could pay my way to school. I used to tell him my aches and pain, my dreams, and aspirations. He would breathe life into my soul and give me hope.

We would write down the things that we needed to achieve in life and by when. He became my prayer partner.

We would ask the caretaker of the church to let us use the church for prayer and fasting which we used to do at least once a month.

My future was dark! We prayed and acted in faith and by faith! Hoping that the God who hears the prayer of two young men will hear and make a way for them, especially for me as Jean Claude already had everything going in his favour.

I am thankful for my dear friend, Jean Claude Dorval who gave me hope. He was to me what Jonathan was to David. I owe him all my gratitude. He was the only one who knew some of my pain and suffering.

I will not forget the day when he told me that his mother sent for him, and he was immigrating to the USA. My heart sank! My stomach hurt! My head felt like it was about to explode.

My best friend and prayer partner was about to leave me in the war-torn zone and poverty-stricken Haiti. Oh, that day was hell! By this time the political unrest of coup d'états and curfews and school closures prevented us from going to school to finish high school and to get our diploma.

I can't recall if his girlfriend had already immigrated to the USA before him, but I could sense that his heart was already there. So, my friend breathed more breath of hope into my life reminding me that God hears and will answer our prayers made at our church, Hebron, during our days of prayer and fasting. I believed him! God did answer our prayers – A few months later, surprisingly, I left Haiti before him. I had applied to study in Jamaica, and I got through. I took my very first flight out of my homeland, Haiti to Jamaica, a flight lasting only 55 minutes in the air, with $200 US in my pocket, from small donations from family and friends to go to West Indies College, now Northern Caribbean University to do my bachelor's degree in theology which would qualify me to work as a pastor in the denominational root of my mother – the Seventh-day Adventist Church. I left not knowing a word in English, except to say, good morning.

As I look back, the odds were very painful and daunting, but they made me a better person today. That's why I am committed to making a positive contribution to alleviate emotional pain and sufferings.

It takes one who was in it to help one who is going through it! I hope I was able to help you in your journey made of odds!

I remember that while my siblings took me to the airport, my brother asked me how I was going to make it in Jamaica to which replied: "God will provide." Indeed, He provided!

As I said, God had it that I left Haiti before my dear friend Jean Claude Dorval. I continued to pray that God would allow his USA green card to come through.

The God that my mother served up to her death to whom she introduced me who became my God, heard my prayer and Jean Claude was able to immigrate to the USA shortly after I went to Jamaica to study.

Just as we prayed and asked God to help me in my dream to become a pastor, Jean Claude's dream was to become an engineer, God blessed us – our dreams were fulfilled just as we prayed. Thanks be to the Almighty God!

Remember, in your pain and suffering, you need to find great friends with whom you can nurture meaningful relationships. It is important to note, to have a friend, you need to be a friend.

The Losers

You can't expect to soar against the odds of life while you are or remain in the company of the losers. It won't work!

The losers will magnify your odds to the point where they will overwhelm you!

They will make your odds bigger than your dreams!

They will use the reality of your present situation to forecast your future success!

They may use your country of origin to determine the breath and length of your intelligence!

They will use the color of your skin to determine the office you can occupy!

They will use your gender to determine your status.

They will use your height to determine your stature.

They will use your level of education to determine your income.

They will use your ocean of fear for the unknown to drown you in the comfort of your present status quo!

They will make you believe that your possibilities are only probabilities therefore it's not worth risking your present discomfort for the unknown.

The irony of your success is that the ones who see you succeed in life, don't know where you are coming from and how hard you had to work to get to where you are today!

They don't know what you went through to get to where you are. They don't know your losses and your pains. Yet, as you start climbing the ladder of success, they don't want to see you at the head. They believe that you are not good enough to have what you have earned. They envy you and they won't stop until they see you are down to nothing or destroyed. They won't mind if you must beg, that will make them feel good! You should not be on par with them or worse doing better than them! Against such, you must wrestle!

It doesn't matter who they are! It doesn't matter what your relationship is to them. You need to stay far away from the losers until they change their attitude about themselves, you, and your future!

If they can't breathe life into you, don't let them suffocate your potential.

Regardless of where you are coming from in life or how deep you are in the ditch, right now, you must change your attitude about life, and you must make something of yourself.

- Deal with your low self-esteem!

- Deal with your emotional bruises!

- Address your unresolved issues!

- Forgive yourself for the things you allowed yourself to get into that may have clipped your wings!

- Forgive others for the things they did to you even if you don't ever have to mention it to them!

- Accept your past failures and mistakes and take full ownership of them!

- Choose to blame no one for the odds in your life!

- Address the fears instilled in you by your past!

- Block the negative voices in your head and replace them with positive ones that will inspire you to success!

- Surround yourself with the right people who can help you pull yourself from under the rubbles of life!

- Therefore, you will soar against the odds!

There is no need for you to fear for the future. The odds will always be present. They were in the past; they are present now and they will be present in the future. You can't escape them, so you must develop a mindset to deal with them.

The way you deal with your present odds will prepare you to deal with bigger and more complex odds effectively and boldly.

The Odds Toughen

When David was in the wilderness tending his father's sheep and goats, he developed something that could have only been offered to him by the odds of the wilderness of life – the ability to fight lions and bear. Something that most of us would dread.

For David, although it was not something that he would have opted for, he accepted it for what it was worth to protect his father's animals against these powerful paws and draws of the wild. It toughened both, his mental and physical strengths.

1 Samuel 17 mentions this theatrical but real scene of David and Goliath. This young shepherd boy was still at the service of the King Saul. His father by now had become an old man, so he was allowed to occasionally return to his father, Jesse to tend to his sheep.

The loving father he was, he sent David on a mission to take food to his three older sons who were in King Saul's army, waiting with fear and in trepidations to fight the well decorated veteran of the camp of the Philistines who drove fear to the Israelites.

Up to that point, David was not known to have had any military skills or training let alone to take on the role of being the savior of such an army as that of the Israelites. At the sight of Goliath, the soldiers fled the scene, but the little shepherd boy stood his ground and believed he was the man for the job. He could take down the well decorated and armoured soldier named Goliath.

The Philistine soldier was well protected by all his army apparatus. His height was frightful as he stood nine feet tall.

At the utterance of his words of confidence in his quest to fight Goliath, David was viewed as conceited, boastful, and incapable of fighting a man like this war veteran. The King himself declared him unfit and too young.

In his defense, he had to rely on the experiences he gained in the wilderness which taught him several things that most of the well experienced soldiers did not have, after all, he had no accolade to place on his curriculum vitae. The only things he had going for him were the following:

- He knew how to use a sling shot!

- He knew that it takes a special skill to kill a lion or a bear!

- He believed in his inner strength!

- He believed in his ability to take down anything!

After all, no one else, up to that time, had killed a bear or a lion with his bare hand and survived to tell the tale – except David!

This kind of advantage could have only been gained by a disadvantaged life offered by daily experiences in the wild. This was the advantage he had over everyone else including King Saul and even Goliath himself.

Despite the negativity around him and about him, he knew that if he believes in his inner abilities, he can conquer anything. He didn't need the armor of the King to do that. He must fight in his own even when his armor or the lack thereof didn't pass the test.

What would happen if only you believed in yourself? Like David, you will conquer the Goliath in your life.

Allow No One To Limit Your Ability

In your quest to soar to higher heights, never allow anyone to limit your ability by what they say or do to you. No infirmities or physical impediments should limit you.

As human beings, our ability doesn't first reside in our "doing" but rather in our "being." It's all in the mind.

We use our hands to write, to feed ourselves and to engage the hands in whatever functions they were programmed to do.

Our feet, to walk and run but we also see others who were born without hands or without feet yet, through the power the mind, they train the body to do what is uncommon, some learn to use their feet to play an instrument, to cook, to feed themselves and to do just about anything someone with all four members would do. When you see such a person with limited mobility or with no mobility doing great performances, we wonder, how did that happen?

It's the power of the mind! This is what you get when you are resilient! This is what you get when you push yourself to the limit – in fact, there is no limit to your inner potential. It only stops where you stop. You determine your own limit. The farther you push yourself, the farther you can go!

The only person who can stop you is *you*!

I like the way Brianna Wiest puts it. In her book: *The Mountain Is You*, she writes:

"There is nothing holding you back in
life more than yourself."[1]

If I must be honest with myself, I must admit that
the moment I look back at the atrocities my father
inflicted on me, I retreat into self-pity and begin to
justify the reasons why I am who I am. This gives me
more reason to sink deeper into the rabbit hole of
blame and victimization.

Similarly, when I catch myself in this act of self-pity
and victim-attitude, I can feel a blanket of sadness and
emotional pain over me which tends to send me back
in time and relive the moments. To mitigate that, I
indulge in self-actualization. Positive reinforcement
that feeds my soul with words of encouragement, and
empowerment to lift me up from the pit of despair.
I rely on reading great books and listening to audiobooks dealing with emotional health to feed my mind
so that I can deal with the unfathomable.

In the words of Brianna Wiest "On the surface,
self-sabotage seems masochistic. It appears to be a
product of self-hatred, low confidence, or a lack of
willpower. Self-sabotage is simply the presence of
an unconscious need that is being fulfilled by self-
sabotage behaviour. We must go through a process
of deep psychological excavation. We must pinpoint

the traumatic event, release unprocessed emotions, find healthier ways to meet our needs, reinvent our self-image, and develop principles such as emotional intelligence and resilience."[1]

As you are reading this book, chances are, the odds might be against you.

From a once aching heart to another, I beg of you not to focus on the odds. You have no control over them, but you have control over how you allow them to affect you. I encourage you to rather focus on the strength within to help you deal with emotional pains. You can't comfortably soar with them! They will hinder your ascent.

Resolve in yourself that you will do whatever needs to be done to deal with your emotional issues. They might be part of the reasons your wings are clipped, and you don't seem to be able to fly the way you were created to.

There are so many people who want you to soar. I am one of them. That's why I wrote this book. Others helped me so it's time for me to return the help!

Soon, it will be time for you to return the help to someone else, but you can't help anyone until you help yourself. Self-care begins with you, and it also ends with you.

We are all different, but I will share with you the things I do to help myself as I soar to higher heights:

- **Self-development and personal growth.** I have a monthly budget for self-development and personal growth. This money I set aside to purchase books and audiobooks on emotional health and healing trauma. It's all about nourishing and nurturing my mind to address the needs of my being. I read at least one book or audiobook per week to help me achieve this. It doesn't have to cost a lot - $25-$50 per month.

- *I write.* I notice that as I read, there is a torrent of knowledge that keeps flowing through my brain cells that propels me to write and to share information and knowledge with others. I also find this is very therapeutic.

- *I exercise.* I consider my body as a gift from God. Therefore, He expects me to take care of it. I can't pray and ask God to bless me with good health unless I am doing my part to promote good health by exercising. He has placed that responsibility squarely at my feet. I must make it my point of duty to exercise at least three times a week for one hour to maintain and or to promote a healthy body. I can't expect God to do for me what He has already done in me.

- *Relationship.* I value and maintain healthy relationships with people who have a positive attitude and help me in my personal growth and development.

- *Diet.* I pay attention to what I eat and my food intake to nourish my body and to maintain a healthy weight.

- *I pray.* I spend time with God who supplies my needs and who gives me strength to deal with the odds of life.

- *Empowering Others.* I invest time in others so that I can help someone take care of their unresolved issues, dream big dreams, and help them with the steps needed to reach their full potential.

- *Financial Contribution.* I contribute financially to worthy causes to help the less fortunate in other parts of the world so that I can help educate a child somewhere else and put food on the table and help them deal with the odds in their own lives.

- *Personal Plans.* I write down the things that I want to accomplish and what I need to do to accomplish them and keep track of my progress.

- *Mindfulness.* I keep myself aware of the hurts that were inflicted on me so that I don't inflict them on others including my wife and my children.

- *Apologies*. If I do anything wrong to someone, including my wife and my children, I exercise humility and acknowledge my faults, apologize, and seek forgiveness.

- *Granting Forgiveness*. I will forgive anyone who did me any wrong or hurt me to ensure that my heart is free from hurts and animosity. This also includes forgiving myself for my own mistakes and shortcomings.

As you are soaring against your own odds, I do hope that this book gave you hope and helped you with your own path to higher heights and emotional health.

Allow the odds of life to be the wind beneath your wings. Let nothing stop you!

So, Soar to the zenith of your potential.

Conclusion

As I shared my painful journey with you, I am thankful for the fact that my sisters, Rosana and Mathurine, along with their families live in New York, USA.

My brother, Ascencio, lives with his family in Quebec, Canada. I live in the Greater Toronto Area, Canada which means that we are just a few hours drive away from each other. We love spending time together just like when we were growing up.

We went through it all but by the grace of the Almighty God, we have made it to be positive contributors to the countries that we now call home, Canada and the USA. It is possible because we also worked hard not to allow the hurts of the past hurt us.

It is my wish and my prayer that, regardless of your past emotional pain, you too will do what needs to be done to ensure that you are not just living but you are thriving in most if not, all areas of your life.

It can only happen if you make it happen!

So, make it happen!

Another Book Written by The Author

THE WILL TO HEAL – Is an emotional health book that takes the readers on a journey into wholeness and a bright future, where dreams come to fruition and lives are changed.

The author uses his skills as a Certified Grief Recovery Specialist and Certified Life Coach to help his readers deal with the unresolved issues of the heart so that they can act on their dreams and aspirations.

Anchored in his faith in God, the author reminds his readers that God created them for greatness. Their dreams must be bigger than their size and God will fit them in overtime.

About This Book

The Unhealed Wounds Of My Father is based on the author's personal experience with childhood trauma and lingering grief which he dealt with well into his adulthood.

The author shares his personal experiences to inspire his readers to go beyond the emotional pains caused by domestic violence inflicted by a spouse, a parent or caregiver.

Emile Maxi uses his experience as a Certified Grief Recovery Specialist and a Certified Life Coach to assist his readers in dealing with their own emotional issues so that they can stop allowing the trauma of the past to deter them from accomplishing their dreams and aspirations.

The author empowers his readers to accept the fact that while bad things may have happened to them, no one can stop them but themselves. Therefore, regardless of the bad, one can't effectively move forward and thrive until they take accountability for holding onto the pain that affected them.

Emile Maxi holds a BA in Theology, an MA in Education, is a Certified Grief Recovery Specialist, and a Certified Life Coach. He has written this book based on his personal experience with childhood trauma and grief in his own life and how he overcame them all.

It's his hope and prayer that through the pages of this book, he will be able to guide his readers to go beyond the pain of trauma and domestic violence so that they can find healing.

He and his wife, June have two young adult daughters.

Notes

Chapter 1

1. Emile Maxi, The Will to Heal, (Altona, Manitoba: Friesen-Press, The Ingram Book Company, 2022), 7.

Chapter 2

1. Ecclesiastes 11:1, 2. NKJV

2. John W. James and Russel Friedman, The Grief Recovery Handbook (New York: Harper-Collins, 2009), 53.

Chapter 3

1. Terrence Real, I Don't Want to Talk About It, (New York: Scribner, 1997), 164.

2. Ibid., 165.

3. Ibid., 165.

4. https://mha.ohio.gov/static/learnandfindhelp/TreatmentServices/TCC/Trauma-Informed-Care-Best-Practices-and-Protocols-for-Domestic-Violence-Programs.pdf

5. Ibid

6. Peter A. Levine and Ann Frederick, Waking the Tiger, Healing Trauma, (California: North Atlantic Books, 1997), 24.

7. Ibid., 24

8. Bessel Van Der Kolk, The Body Keeps the Score, (New York, NY: Penguin Books, 2015), 102-103.

Chapter 4

1. John W. James and Russel Friedman, The Grief Recovery Handbook (New York: Harper-Collins, 2009), 78.

2. John C. Maxwell, Developing the Leader Within You 2.0 (Nashville, TN: Harper Collins Leadership, 2018), 2.

3. Brianna Wiest, The Mountain Is You, (Brooklyn, NY: Thought Catalog Books, 2020), 7.

Chapter 5

1. Phillip Newton, Guide and Workbook: Healing from Childhood Trauma, (Alberta, Canada: Amazon.ca, 2021), 33.

Chapter 6

1. Mike Baker, Best Self. Be You, Only Better (New York, NY: DEY ST.; 2019), 11.

2. Amanda Dewinter, The Success Code – Unlocking Your Potential, Achieve Your Goals (London: UK, HQ: Harper Collins Publishers Ltd, 2021), 34.

Chapter 7

1. John C. Maxwell, The 21 Irrefutable Laws of Leadership, 10th Edition (Nashville, TN: Harper Collins Leadership, 2007), 11.

2. Job 13:15 (KJV)

3. Jeremiah 29:11 (NIV)

4. Isaiah 43:2 (NIV)

5. Philippians 4:6-7 (NIV)

6. Jennie Allen, Get Out Of Your Head, (USA: Colorado Springs: Waterbrook, 2020), 112.

Chapter 8

1. Andrew L. Blackwood, The Art of a Genuine Apology, (Nexus And Serenity Publishing, Toronto: ON, Canada, 2017), 146.

2. Victor J. Strecher, Life On Purpose, (New York, NY: Harper One, 2016), 23.

3. Ibid., 23

Chapter 9

1. Brené Brown, Rising Strong, (New York, NY: Random House, 2017), 253.

2. 1 Samuel 15:35 (NLT)

3. 1 Samuel 16:13 (NLT)

Chapter 10

1. Brianna Wiest, The Mountain Is You, (Brooklyn, NY: Thought Catalog Books, 2020), 11.

Printed in the USA
CPSIA information can be obtained
at www.ICGtesting.com
CBHW031923221024
16238CB00011B/200

9 781038 315748